DRUMMING TO THE BEAT
OF A DIFFERENT MARCHER

Finding the Rhythm for Teaching
A Differentiated Classroom

By Debbie Silver

Incentive Publications, Inc.
Nashville, Tennessee

Acknowledgement
For their unconditional love and support I would like to thank
my Thompson family, my children (Scott, Maverick, Stephanie,
Andy, Jeremy, Kandy, and Kit), and my husband/best friend,
Lawrence Silver. You are my touchstones and a constant source
of joy. Also, welcome to the world, Charlotte Abigail Pace.

Illustrated by Marta Drayton
Cover by Kristi Jones
Edited by Jennifer J. Streams and Charlotte Bosarge

Library of Congress Control Number 2002112408
ISBN 0-86530-584-6

PRINTED IN THE UNITED STATES OF AMERICA
www.incentivepublications.com

Table of Contents

Introduction

"If a man does not keep pace with his companions, perhaps it is because he hears a different drummer. Let him step to the music which he hears, however measured or far away."

—Henry David Thoreau

It wasn't until I started school that I realized just how different the drummer I heard was. I vividly remember my very first day of school. Mrs. Castleberry, my teacher, asked us six-year-olds to color a worksheet picture of an apple. I dutifully pulled out my two favorite crayons, green and blue, and laboriously tried to get large chunks of colored wax to stay within the confines of the fruit outline centered on the paper. Not being blessed with fine motor skills, my strokes made their way beyond the boundaries of the paper itself.

I was quite pleased with my final product—until a dismayed Mrs. C. held up my paper for everyone to see and pronounced: "Boys and girls, look at this. First of all, apples are NOT blue and green. But more importantly, I said to 'color in the apple,' and look what Debbie did . . . she went outside the lines!" With a grand show of dismay she wadded up my paper and tossed it in the trash. I can still remember the collective "uh-oh's" as other students quickly tried to conform their masterpieces to her expectations.

We soon learned that there was to be no "going outside the lines" that year! We were led through a tedious nine-month term of being quiet, sitting still, and repeating exactly what we were told to do. It was not a good year. As one who never made it out of the "Slug Group" (or whatever insipid name she used for the low readers) I found myself constantly feeling like something was wrong with me. While some of the students were able to satisfy Mrs. Castleberry's every directive, I was just thankful that I remembered to change my pajama bottoms for real clothes before I showed up at school. I knew the drum I heard was indeed "distant and far away," but rather than learning to cherish my "outside the lines" thinking, I felt ashamed and frustrated. I remember sitting on the back row thinking, "But I'm smart, too!"

The good news is that there have always been some teachers, and later I had some of them, who have the perception, the imagination, and the courage it takes to go beyond the traditional teacher-centered model. They are able to look inside children and see not only their unique gifts, but also to use those gifts for engaging, for motivating, and for challenging. Instead of having us march to their personal, inflexible beats, they encourage us to find our own ways, our own rhythms, our own strengths. They are able to teach us by recognizing and utilizing the gifts we already have. This book is dedicated to all those teachers who do indeed drum to the beat of their different marchers, and it is written for all those who wish they could.

"Beat of a Different Marcher"

By Debbie Silver & Monte Selby

Bobby marches to the beat of his different drummers
Jeffrey does his reading, but he can't do numbers
Shawna's up and talkin' 90 miles an hour, again
Can't find his book or pencil, that would be Ben
Hyperactive, dyslexic, class clown, non-reader
Upper class, no class, off-task, bottom feeder
Little Arty's a challenge; Martin's a dream
We've seen them all, they all need to be seen.

        All children in reach when we find their rhythm—
        The step, the dance, the song within them
        That's a better journey, but so much harder
        Too extraordinary, but so much smarter
        To drum to the beat of each different marcher.

Sandy's in the slow group, a proven low achiever
She's the small quiet one, not a class leader
Crayons in her hand, she can draw what she knows best
But no room for pictures on the standardized test.
Ballerina, bricklayer, biochemist, ball player
Diesel driver, drum major, diva-destined, dragon slayer—
Some kids have a chance, with a different choice
To show what they know, they must have a voice.

All children in reach when we find their rhythm—
The step, the dance, the song within them
That's a better journey, but so much harder
Too extraordinary, but so much smarter
To drum to the beat of each different marcher.

Introspective, oversized, minimized, criticized
Round holes, square lives, not much room for compromise.
There's a new song not yet written
For each and every child, will we listen?

All children in reach when we find their rhythm—
The step, the dance, the song within them
That's a better journey, but so much harder
Too extraordinary, but so much smarter
To drum to the beat of each different marcher.
Let's all dance to the beat of each different marcher!

Keeping Pace
(Getting Started)

Dealing with classroom management issues is always a key concern for new teachers as well as those trying to find better ways to create a thriving learning environment. Chapter 1 offers different perspectives on classroom management as well as many insights about how practiced teachers do it.

Keeping pace with individual students is far more expedient and successful when parents are part of the process. Chapter 2 is a guide to getting parents involved and keeping them involved, while not letting them overpower the school's mission or authority. Activities for helping parents deal with their children are included.

PART 1
Keeping Pace (Getting Started)

Chapter 1 Classroom Management
If They Would Just Get These KIDS Out of My Room, I Could Probably Do My Job!

Chapter 2 Parental Involvement
If It Weren't for the Parents, We Wouldn't Have All These Kids in the First Place!

Classroom Management

If They Would Just Get These KIDS
Out of My Room,
I Could Probably Do My Job!

Do Whatever Works!

Keeping pace with a classroom full of diverse marchers first requires that a teacher become acquainted with his or her own distant drummer. It is important that teachers learn to trust their "inner voice" and use it as a guiding principle for all that they do. It is vital early on to get a sense of self and a sense of purpose.

I often say that my philosophy of teaching can be summed up in two words: "Whatever works!" Now be very careful about how this philosophy is interpreted: I am most definitely NOT talking about stop-gap measures, arbitrary decisions, or short-term solutions.

I used to show my Classroom Management class this cartoon:

"Tommy, I guess you have just earned yourself 10 minutes with Mr. Rattles!!"

My students roar when they see it. Then I ask them, "Would that discipline technique work?" They, of course, tell me that it isn't feasible, not humane, not legal, and so forth. Again I ask, "But would it work?" They usually get a stunned look on their faces and answer that it would, indeed, work. Then I ask them what they mean by the term "work." Usually they say, "Well, I'll bet Tommy won't misbehave anymore." My response is that if stopping Tommy's inappropriate behavior was the only goal, then I guess you could say it worked.

Making Tommy behave is just one outcome of the many things teachers must consider when making classroom decisions. It is vital that, as quickly as possible, a teacher formulate what he or she believes about the purpose of education and the long-term goals she or he hopes to achieve with students.

The teacher in the cartoon would probably nip Tommy's behavior in the bud, but has she promoted a classroom that is a caring community? Has she advanced Tommy's requisite knowledge skills? Has she helped Tommy become a contributing member of society? Nope! Then she is going to have to think of something else. I know this is an extreme example, but it holds true for all teacher decisions including those made about what is put in the classroom, how things are arranged, all of the ambient touches added, how rules and consequences are set up, attire, the structure of lesson plans, assessment techniques, and virtually everything that has to do with how a teacher chooses to teach.

It took me 10 years of trying various techniques to find a method I really liked for getting the attention of students who were busily working in small groups. I tried counting backwards, flipping the light switch, and whispering. None of those methods was satisfactory for me. I finally discovered the perfect solution in a toy store! I bought a child's xylophone. It makes a soothing, calming sound, and it gets the attention of everyone immediately! I've been using it ever since—even for my university students. I know it sounds like a little thing, but it has really improved my classroom environment; it "works" for me. I just wish I had thought of it sooner.

Lion Taming 101

Despite common assumptions, a teacher does not have to greet students on the first day with a frown, a whip, and an upraised chair in order to establish order and discipline (even if all the other teachers are doing it). Students are much better served by a teacher who greets them at the door, shows them to their assigned seats, and gets them started on an assignment. Teachers can even smile while doing all that.

This chapter describes some of the key elements for teachers to consider when planning classroom management strategies. Classroom management is about much more than discipline techniques; it is about everything teachers do in the classroom. It is important that each teacher let his or her own classroom management style continually evolve until he or she learns what works. Even learning what not to do ever again is beneficial. (Like the time I jokingly suggested to a very literal student that for his consequence he should, "go play on the little yellow line on the highway in front of the school." Thankfully I caught him before he made it out of the front gate!)

When I say to "do whatever works" I am, of course, not only talking about short-term goals but also the life-long outcomes. I truly believe that every teacher should learn to trust his or her own "distant drummer." As a person who has power with children, it is a teacher's obligation to ensure that every decision and action is consistent with what students should know and be like (or are on their way to becoming) when they leave the classroom.

I must be honest and confess that I have probably made every mistake there is to make in managing a classroom. Over the years, I have fluctuated from managing by mood swings (mine) to a diligent application of Lee Canter's Assertive Discipline techniques to Alfie Kohn's absolute classroom democracy plan. None of these systems *totally* worked for me. However, I did learn from all of them. Talking with other educators and reading about alternative management strategies has helped me reevaluate what I do in my own classes and has given me many new ideas to try.

All teachers learn as they go along. Be patient. It takes more than a year or two to find a personalized path. Some say it takes 3 to 5 years for most teachers to "hit their stride." Teaching is, after all, a faithful work of art and work of heart.

It is necessary that teachers figure out who they are, determine a mission, and set up a classroom conducive to these goals. All of those elements are essential to a management plan. Ultimately, a classroom management plan should be a well-thought-out system that is grounded in recognized behavioral theory. It should be crafted to meet both the short-range goal of having a class run smoothly and the long-range goals of having students become self-sufficient, successful life-long learners who will become contributing community members.

We will call the associated teacher behaviors *The Ten C's*.

The 10 C's of Classroom Management

Effective classroom managers are:

1. Competent
2. Cognizant
3. Communicative
4. Confident
5. Constructive
6. Calm
7. Consistently Fair
8. Caring
9. Contemplative
10. Courageous

1. Be Competent

At one time I believed that it was impossible to run an effective classroom without a carefully crafted set of three to five rules. Now, having visited hundreds of classrooms, I have changed that notion. I have been in some highly successful classrooms where there are either no stated rules or the "rules" are actual governing principles like (1) Be respectful, and (2) Do your best. I have seen master teachers who are able to foster such a caring community and such a positive learning environment that rules are replaced with implied standards of behavior and established social mores. To me this is the ideal.

However, for those of us still on the path to becoming a true master, for those who are struggling with difficult students, and for those who are just beginning the journey, I still believe that a written set of rules can be a good place to start. While there is debate among theorists and educators about the desirability of having a highly structured assertive discipline plan, there is general agreement that effective classroom rules will:

- address classroom behavior, not academics

- be applied to all students at all times

- be limited to no more than five in number

- address only the most important behaviors

- be specific and observable

- have logical, consistent consequences

- be reinforced with positive recognition

In his book *7 Habits of Highly Effective People*, Stephen Covey advises that when setting out on a new course of action, one should "begin with the end in mind." This is particularly relevant to classroom management plans.

First: As teachers craft a plan, it is important to ensure that each rule, each consequence, and each reward is consistent with the long-range goals for students.

Second: If using an assertive teacher-centered plan to regain control of an unruly class (or to help establish a teacher as a new classroom manager), consider moving away from it as soon as it is comfortable to do so.

As the teacher becomes more confident and more competent, he or she can aim at building a classroom community that shares more control with students. After all, isn't the ultimate purpose of a discipline plan to help the students develop self-discipline?

> *The only way to have true power is to give some of it away.*

Inexperienced teachers or teachers who are new to a school need to remember to read every word of the school and district handbooks! Highlight important parts and keep them handy. As an employee, a teacher is bound by these guidelines, and it is crucial to understand both the stated and unstated implications of these documents. Beginners will be helped by consulting experienced teachers and/or administrators who can provide feedback on ideas for a classroom management plan or help resolve a conflict with policy or an unforeseen outcome that a new teacher may overlook.

When developing an individual and distinct way of dealing with students, be aware that others may not share those views. "Hearing a different marcher" is fine, but a thorough understanding of the issues involved in establishing a positive classroom environment will help teachers defend their choices. I once had an administrator who totally supported classical conditioning as a management technique. He thought that behavior modification was the only way to run a classroom. I had grown to feel that rewarding approved behavior was a bit manipulative and self-serving. Because I keep current with my professional reading, I was able to cite experts who supported my beliefs.

Sometimes it also takes a little humor to ease your way: I think what ultimately convinced him to let me do it my way was this poem I wrote and placed on his desk.

Ode to Ivan Pavlov
by Debbie Pace (Silver)

Oh, Ivan you pervade each day
Within my classroom walls—
With one bell ring the students start
Out bounding for the halls.

Conditioning can't be denied
As classic as the text,
Just smelling of the lunchroom food
Will trigger gag reflex.

Mere mention of the "homework" word
Brings on collective bleats.
Appearances by principals
Cause hearts to skip their beats.

You'd think that they'd remember you,
Your work describes them so,
But children learn in unique ways,
As you of all should know.

So Ivan, I apologize
That when their memory jogs
Their best recall of Pavlov is . . .
"The guy with 'slobbering dogs'?"

A competent teacher is well-informed both about his or her subject area and about how best to deal with his or her students. A prepared teacher stays up-to-date by reading educational literature, attending workshops, and continually building a repertoire of skills and resources. Expert teachers constantly strive to improve their knowledge base and seek to grow towards an even higher level of competence.

2. Be Cognizant

Being cognizant means being aware. Often teachers cause their own discipline problems by acts of omission as much as acts of commission. It is not that teachers are uncaring or that they set out purposefully to provoke children, it is that many times teachers are simply not conscious of what they are doing (or not doing). Work on being observant of everything going on in the classroom. Be aware of what students are doing as well as what they are likely to do. This knowledge can be one of a teacher's greatest management assets. A teacher who is alert to potential problems can head them off before they ever start. Call it being proactive, taking preventive measures, being "with it," or whatever—but do it!

Assigning Seats

Once the classroom is set up in a way to maximize student attention and minimize off-task behavior, the next order of business is to assign seats. For whole-group instruction do not let the students choose their own seats. On the first day students arrive have them sit in assigned seats (can be random or alphabetical to help you learn their names). Make folded placards, lay name strips out, or have the seating arrangement posted where everyone can see it. Definitely have it already planned to control where they sit. Tell them they will be sitting at that place only a few days until you get to know them.

After developing a feel for who the students are, reassign their seats. (I take at least as much time filling out my seating charts as I do preparing a lesson plan.) Experiment with different combinations until every student has been given a maximum opportunity to succeed. Angle friendly talkers as well as bitter enemies out of each other's line of sight. Surround particularly argumentative students with several quiet, self-possessed ones. This placement ritual is very cathartic, and it gives teachers a chance to reflect on what's going on with their students.

Whenever changing the seating arrangement use the magic words "for now" with students. Say something like "These will be your new seats for now. We will be changing seats again in _____ weeks. If you are unhappy about your seating assignment, you can write me a note in your journal, but this is your seat for now. Let's begin our activity . . ."

Each teacher will have to judge how often to rearrange seating. A rule of thumb is the younger the students, the more often changes are needed. High school students are usually okay with the same seats for one grading period. Middle and intermediate students thrive well with changes every 4 to 6 weeks. Let the students know that there is nothing punitive about seating reassignments, it's just beneficial to move them around so they will have a chance to interact with different people. Some teachers never change students' seats because they think it's too much trouble. Actually, they are missing a golden opportunity to redistribute the power structure in their rooms, take care of minor annoyances, and promote student involvement.

Don't sit; move!

It is important for teachers to know what is going on among their students. Make sure the seating arrangement allows accessibility to all students as he or she monitors, teaches, recognizes, and affirms individuals. Have students keep traffic lanes uncluttered. Move in an easy, non-threatening manner to different areas of the room at different times. Also, move in unpredictable directions. This allows a teacher to re-engage a dreamer or a drowsy student by moving close to that student and asking a direct question about the lesson.

Students who are trying to confront one another may be glaring at each other. Students may be trying to speak to or entertain one another. Step between them and purposefully engage one or both of them in the lesson.

One of a teacher's best proactive measures is to be able to "move in on" students readily. A lot of acting out can be stopped before it starts by standing close to a student and speaking quietly to her or him. Teachers who are standing and moving around have a much better idea about how well a lesson and a classroom community is really going.

Watch Their Eyes!

This one seems obvious, but many teachers fail to make direct eye contact with students. More can be learned about what is going on in a room and with students if a teacher focuses on their eyes. Stand outside the door each time there is a class change. Greet students as they walk in the room. Make eye contact. If a student seems angry or distressed ask her/him to wait in the hall for a moment. While other students are in the room doing their sponge activity (bell work assignment) take a brief moment to find out if the student is going to be able to function in class. It is possible to de-escalate a lot of acting out by showing concern and offering to let the student "cool off" before entering the classroom.

Be Have!

"I'm going to tell you what I want you to do in just two words . . ."

Facilitate lessons by making eye contact to keep students involved. Pay attention to what they are watching. If there is contraband (I know what you're thinking, but I'm just talking about school contraband—gum, candy, water guns, cheat sheets, etc.) the students will know where it is, and so does the teacher who watches their eyes.

If students are behaving inappropriately, capture their attention by looking directly at them. Sometimes no words are needed to redirect their actions; it can all be done with eyes and a slight movement of the head or hand. (One note about eye contact: In some Native American and Eastern cultures children are taught that it is disrespectful to make direct eye contact with a superior. Be mindful of that and other cultural anomalies when working with children who have different traditions.)

> *The eyes are the windows to the soul.*

Be Knowledgeable about Why Students Misbehave

Learn all you can about the developmental stages of the students you teach. Some things that students do are simply actions associated with their particular age group. Things like giggling, sulking, acting bored, fidgeting, and other minimally disturbing behavior patterns are typical during certain growth stages.

Understanding the normal phases of the age group being taught will help a teacher to be more patient with conduct issues. And, if you think these attributes are particular only to students, check out those who are giggling, sulking, fidgeting, and acting bored at the next faculty meeting. Be aware that most inappropriate behavior can be attributed to four main causes, and most of the time those causes are preventable.

Catherine Watson (1995) states that the reasons for student misbehavior are:

1) to gain power

2) to get attention

3) to seek revenge

4) to avoid failure

As you move towards a classroom that is more democratic, students will automatically gain more power. Part 2 of this book deals with encouraging positive group dynamics, differentiating instruction, giving students more choices about their learning, and engaging all learners. Chapter 7 discusses how to actively promote emotional literacy. These instructional strategies will go a long way towards helping students feel empowered, giving them an appropriate outlet for the attention they need, and helping them avoid failure.

Watson's third reason is a little more complicated. If a student who misbehaves because she or he is seeking revenge, the teacher has a serious dilemma. Either this is a student who is extremely troubled or there is definitely something amiss in the classroom management plan. Teachers should behave towards students in a manner that in no way leads to feelings of revenge-seeking in a normal child. The teacher's role is that of the protagonist, not the antagonist.

Teachers of regular education students who manifest the need to "get even" with a student need to take a hard look at what they (the teachers) are doing to trigger such feelings. Obviously there is a deeper problem than just normal "acting out." It may be that the teacher and the student should meet with a third party to discuss the problem. (Teachers of students who have been identified as emotional behavior disordered [E.B.D.] or other such exceptionalities are more likely to encounter this phenomenon and should have special training to deal with it when it happens).

Being cognizant of everything going on is described by some researchers as "with-it-ness." Being "with-it" is an attribute that has been linked to effective teaching (Kounin, 1977). Teachers who are "with it" deter small infractions before they become large ones (the ripple effect). They target the responsible party(ies) causing the distraction and quickly redirect the attention back to the lesson. Good classroom managers are alert, attentive, and able to act quickly.

"No, I have not had too much caffeine, I am just very VERY alert!"

3. Be Communicative

Being able to communicate on all levels with students is crucial to effective classroom management. Teachers who want successful classrooms take time during the first few days of school to teach basic understandings (limits and courteous behavior). They realize that students come to them with different experiences, expectations, and even cultural norms. Often when a student commits some perceived breach of etiquette it is not a result of insubordination, but rather a lack of understanding about what was expected. In the South, we routinely teach our children to address their elders by the terms "'Ma'am" and

Drumming to the Beat of a Different Marcher

"Sir." Children who transfer into our schools from other parts of the country are often misinterpreted as rude or defiant because this custom is not something they normally do.

Communicative teachers go over procedures and routines (some call them rituals) in great detail to ensure that all students understand the expectations. In the book, *Discipline with Dignity*, authors Curwin and Mendler suggest that teachers give tests over behavioral expectations. They tie class privileges to making a perfect score on the test and continue giving the test to those who have not yet made 100%. Eventually they all do. Taking time to assess students' understanding of the expected behaviors not only reinforces the "ground rules" it provides written documentation that the student heard and understood what was expected. (Keep that documentation handy for warding off lawsuits from those future lawyers you are now teaching!)

Communicative teachers talk about procedures, demonstrate them, model them, practice them, and revisit them when necessary. Despite what I wrote in the Ivan Pavlov poem, I always taught my students that bells were my signals not theirs. Never let students think that bells, announcements, or departures of other classes dismisses them; the teacher is the one who says when the class is over. On the first day (or any day if something is a problem) stop. Go over it again. Get it right. Otherwise, it will not get better until the teacher gets better.

Examples of typical classroom procedures:
- lining up for lunch, recess, dismissal, etc.
- drills (fire, tornado, intruder)
- distributing and collecting materials and assignments
- sharpening pencils
- using the bathroom
- tardies
- lunch count
- specialty procedures like setting up musical instruments, booting up computers, and working in the lab.

When discussing class rules, customs, or standards, effective managers take special care to talk with students about why the policies are in effect. They actively listen to the concerns and opinions of their students. They give their students a voice in the way the class is run.

It is important to note that written rules are not the only way students get messages about what is expected. They watch everything their teacher says and does. Teachers get desired behavior from students by communicating clear expectations to them and following up.

Some teachers still believe that in order to get compliance from children, they have to be unpleasant. Nothing could be further from the truth. At no time should a teacher be aggressive or mean-spirited. Maintain an orderly classroom by communicating in a warm, friendly, and assertive manner. The toughest part for most new teachers is being assertive.

Assertive and aggressive are not the same thing. Aggressive means combative, belligerent, and hostile. All aggressive actions are inappropriate in a classroom setting (for faculty as well as students). Assertive means forthright, definite, and positive. When a teacher gives students definitive expectations and consistently demonstrates that he or she means what is said, the students will respond positively.

"This about sums up my classroom management plan."

Some teachers lament, "Well, I have my rules clearly displayed so that everyone can see them, and the students still don't pay any attention to them!" My answer is that it takes more than writing the rules to get the message across. Inform, model, practice, and continually reinforce the rule if you want it followed.

I was doing a clinical supervision with a novice teacher who had asked me to help her understand why her students did not follow the rules she had on the board. She confided that she used one of the same rules I did: "Students will follow directions the first time they are given," and yet her students wouldn't comply. I sat in the back of her room and observed the following interactions:

Miss Wiseman *(standing in the front of the room with a big smile while students are talking and settling in):* Hi, class! We are going to have a terrific lesson today on what causes an eclipse. Everyone open your book to page 64.

Kit *(turning around after talking to a friend during the directions, asking Miss Wiseman loudly):* What page?

Miss Wiseman *(patiently):* Page 64.

Nicole *(speaking loudly to classmate across two rows):* What page did she say?

Miss Wiseman *(answering for the classmate):* I said page 64. *(She walks over to Nicole's desk and helps her find the page. She then glances around at students still fumbling through their materials. She resignedly walks back to the front of the room and holds up her book for them to see).* Students, this is the page I want you to find. *(She waits a beat.)* Has everyone found the page?

Mackenzie: I forgot my book.

Miss Wiseman *(becoming frustrated):* Okay, then share with Andre. Now . . . *(She is interrupted by a loud scraping sound as Mackenzie noisily scoots her chair over to Andre's desk.)*

Brian *(remarking to another student):* That's not the right page, you nimrod, we skipped that chapter, remember?

Miss Wiseman *(now really quite agitated):* Okay, everyone, STOP! Hold up your hand if you have found page 64 and are ready to go on. I'll wait until all hands are raised . . .

And so it went. Approximate time for Miss Wiseman to start her lesson was 6 minutes.

During our follow-up meeting I handed Miss Wiseman my scripting notes. I had written only times, dialogue, and actions; there were no evaluative comments. I asked her to look over the script to see if she detected any patterns that might be enlightening. After reading over the events I recorded, she stared at me wide-eyed and said, "I told them to get on page 64 too many times, didn't I?" I let her continue. "I guess if I really want them to listen I should say things just once. But if I do that, some of them will never be on the right page when we start!"

I am sure you picked up on the problem right away, didn't you? Even though her rule about following directions was prominently written and clearly spoken, Miss Wiseman's words, actions, and tone clearly communicated to her students that she had no expectation of their being able to comply. So many times teachers undermine their own authority by not communicating in every way that they expect students to do what is asked.

It is imperative that teachers tell students about their plan and its purpose. Generally, if a rule is stated, there will be a logical consequence for breaking the rule. Assume that Miss Wiseman's classroom management plan stated that the first rule infraction would mean a check mark by the student's name (as a warning); the second rule infraction would mean a second check mark (two checks = one journal page assignment), and so on.

Now let's assume that Miss Wiseman has already thoroughly discussed her rules and the reasons they are in place. She has explained that her underlying goal is to be sure that in no case will any student be allowed to stop the learning process for others. The purpose of the rule about following directions the first time they are given is to help students take responsibility for their own learning, and to keep the learning process from being interrupted for others.

When they practice the rule about following directions, Miss Wiseman clarifies that if on occasion a student quietly asks for help from another student, or silently moves over to share a book with someone, it will not be breaking the spirit of the rule.

However, if a student speaks out or in any way disrupts the lesson, the rule is clearly broken. The students practice appropriate ways to get help without disturbing others. Then the encounter might go something like this:

Miss Wiseman *(standing in the front of the room with a big smile, and pausing until everyone is facing forward and attentive)*: Hi, everyone! We are going to have a terrific lesson today on what causes an eclipse. Please open your book to page 64. *(She pauses just long enough to give the students time to find the page in their books.)*

Kit *(loudly)*: What page?

(Miss Wiseman looks directly at Kit. She lets him see that she is making a check mark by his name on her clipboard. She does not answer the interruption. She goes on with her teaching.)

(Kit realizes what has happened and quickly looks over to another's student's book to find the page they are on.)

Nicole *(whispering quietly to a classmate)*: What page did she say? *(Classmate silently shows her the page, and they both are ready to begin.)*

(Miss Wiseman goes on with her teaching.)

(Mackenzie quietly scoots her chair over to a classmate's desk to look on with him.)

(Miss Wiseman asks the class a question about the picture on page 64; all students are engaged in the activity.)

Approximate time for Miss Wiseman to start her lesson—25 seconds. If Miss Wiseman's goal is to have students behave responsibly rather than just obediently (and hopefully it is), she should be very happy with the previous scenario.

- Do not begin instruction until all students are focused and attentive.

- Be sure your voice and body language are consistent with your words.

- Use direct eye contact and simple hand gestures to redirect off-task or inappropriate behavior.

- Use close proximity and a quiet voice to make reminders and censures personal and private.

- Be warm and friendly, and be firm.

- Talk to upset students away from other students.

- Practice active listening skills.

- Write emails, notes, or letters to students occasionally just to tell them why you are glad that you are their teacher.

4. Be Constructive

School is about building up, not tearing down. Whatever is included in a discipline plan, the positive recognition procedures will be its most important feature. Certainly teachers have to limit choices, attend to disruptive behavior, and ensure that the learning process is interrupted as little as possible. A no-nonsense firm approach is often needed in such instances. Not everything said and done has to be bright and cheery, but there are a lot of positive, proactive things that can be done to keep a class running smoothly. Just as teachers respond better to affirmative comments than negative remarks, so do students.

Many elementary teachers encourage their future students by sending them welcoming letters before school ever starts. I've known middle school sports teachers who sent Welcome Back postcards to all the pupils on their teams. Some of the most effective teachers I know call parents to report when good things are going on with their children. Effective classroom managers find ways to give students positive recognition on a regular basis.

One of my favorite methods for affirming my students is to write a note or letter to them. I've had students who shrugged off my spoken positive comments and praise, but I have yet to have a student return a positive message I have written. For some students my letter is the first such affirmation they have ever received from an adult. Sometimes I thank a child for a specific action like helping a struggling classmate or backing off from a fight. Other times I tell them that I noticed how hard they are trying or how much their work or behavior has improved. Still other times I tell them what potential I see in them or how glad I am to be their teacher.

If the note is sincere and specific, even the most unreceptive students will think about and appreciate what it says.

Tips for Writing to Students

- Write things that are positive and specific to the individual student. (Some students will compare their messages from you to see if you wrote the same thing to two different people.)

- Make sure everyone gets at least one note from you during the year.

- Be truthful and be sincere. You can even be funny if that's how you interact with students, but be very careful that your words cannot be misinterpreted as sarcastic or negative (humor is tricky without facial expressions and vocal tone to indicate that you are joking).

- Make sure your positive comments have "no strings attached."

- Don't make a big deal of presenting the note. Be as private as possible (you can even leave it in a locker or mail it).

- Don't ask the student if he or she read the note; give it freely, and let it go.

- Don't ask for, or expect, anything in return.

Chapter 7 deals with the importance of the words we both say and write to students, and it discusses attribution theory and emotional literacy. For now, let me just caution you on the amount of praise a teacher uses. I learned the hard way that too much praise creates a "praise junky!" If praise is effusive or indiscriminate, it loses its value to students.

Personally, I'm a really positive and verbal person and I truly enjoy giving others tributes as well as expressing my appreciation. (I even praise people I don't know. The other day at the airport I told one of the security screeners, "Thank you for helping that lady with her bag. Your mother would be very proud of you." He immediately called for a drug dog check on me.) The point is that in my classroom my constant compliments soon lost their value. Towards the end of the year my students would say things like, "Oh, you say that to everybody," or "I'm not going to ask Ms. Silver for her opinion because she likes everything!" It's not easy to find the right balance, but you'll learn to do what works best for you and your students.

Another warning about praise is that it's self-serving to tie praise to a teacher's approval of what the student does or does not do. Statements like "I'm so proud of you," "I love the way you followed my directions," and "I like the way Tiffany Renee is sitting quietly," subtly tell the children that their goal should be to please the teacher. Just a slight shift of phrasing can give a positive message and help students learn to find approval within themselves and from adults other than their teacher. The above statements could be changed to "I imagine you feel really good that your hard work paid off." "I'll bet most of you discovered that when you followed directions it made the assignment a lot easier!" "Those of you who are sitting quietly will want to tell your parents how well you listened today."

Along that same line, there is a great deal of argument these days over whether or not teachers should reinforce positive behavior with extrinsic rewards. Purists say that students need to find intrinsic value in the work itself and that "paying them off" teaches them to work for the reward rather than drawing joy from the experience alone. They cite studies which indicate that intrinsically rewarding behaviors can actually be extinguished if behavior is re-rewarded over a period of time, after which the reward is removed.

One school of thought argues that anything a teacher does externally to reward student behavior not only robs the student of the natural consequences of his or her choice, it diminishes the student's ability to make independent decisions and robs her or him of the inherent joy of the experience. On the other side of the argument, it is suggested that teachers have a purposeful, highly visible system of rewarding student choices which are positive (i.e. pleasing to the teacher).

There are reasonable viewpoints advanced by those on both sides. However, there were absolutes on both sides that did not ring true for me. For instance, I am NOT going to teach without smiling, patting, or praising! And I am NOT going to have a no-discretion, no-brain, no-tolerance policy about students being in their seats before the bell rings.

What Are Rewards?

Extrinsic rewards: Rewards that come from an outside source such as the teacher. Extrinsic rewards include the obvious bonuses such as prizes, certificates, special privileges, gold stars, stickers, candy, gum, redeemable tokens, grades, or even money. Teacher praise is also considered to be an extrinsic reward as are more subtle signs of approval such as "thumbs up" signals: smiles, nods, hugs, and pats on the back.

Intrinsic rewards: Rewards such as the inherent or natural consequences of the behavior. Some researchers prefer the term "reinforcers" to the term "rewards" because teachers use them to strengthen, or reinforce, behavior, therefore making it more likely to be repeated.

Task-contingent rewards: Rewards that are available to students for merely participating in an activity without regard to any standard of performance (e.g. a sticker for anyone who turns in a homework paper).

Performance-contingent rewards: Rewards that are available only when the student achieves a certain standard (e.g., a sticker for anyone who makes at least 95% on a homework assignment).

Success-contingent rewards: Rewards that are given for good performance and that might reflect either success or progress towards a goal (e.g. a sticker for anyone who has at least 95% on a homework paper, or who improves his or her last score by at least 10%).

Most researchers agree that task-contingent rewards are at best futile and at worst counterproductive. There are varying opinions about the need for either performance-contingent or success-contingent rewards.

5. Be Calm

Once while I was teaching in a large elementary/middle school, I was asked to be a hall monitor during a special Saturday event. Parts of the school had been locked to keep students and visitors out of unsupervised areas. As I did one of my walk-throughs I spotted 4 students in an off-limits area. I knew one of them to be a notorious troublemaker and I called for them to stop. When they heard me, they ran. I hurried after them calling more loudly for them to stop. They continued to run, which infuriated me. Despite the fact that I was wearing high heels, I started running full speed after them. I'm quite sure they enjoyed our little chase all over the building because I could hear them laughing.

Finally they got outside and ran into the crowd. I was furious! I stormed into the school office and started yelling that "We have to get those students, NOW!" I was red-faced, out of breath, and out of control.

My principal, who was talking to some parents, excused herself, took me into her office, and asked me to sit down. I was almost hyperventilating at that point. My principal said, "It seems we have a problem."

"Yes," I gasped. "We've got to find those kids NOW!"

"I'm not worried about the kids right now, Ms. Silver, I'm worried about you!"

"Oh, I'll be okay as soon as I get my breath!" I huffed.

"You misunderstand," she said calmly. "I'm worried about how you have chosen to handle this incident. You were running down the halls yelling, then you came into the office and were very unprofessional in front of parents, and now you look as if you are ready to do harm to some of our students."

I was stunned. I was hurt. I was humiliated. I sputtered a moment and then said, "But they were where they weren't supposed to be!"

"I realize that."

"And when I called to them, they wouldn't come!"

"Uh-huh."

"And when I tried to reach them, they ran away!"

"And what did you do at that point?"

"I chased them."

"Why?"

"Because they ran!"

She gently put her arm on my shoulder and said, "Ms. Silver, would you be able to identify any of the students?"

I nodded.

"And do you not think that it is highly likely they will be here Monday when we get back to school?"

I didn't say anything.

"And don't you think you could have saved yourself a lot of energy and a lot of embarrassment if you had just written down the names of the students you knew and locked the door behind them?"

She was right, of course. I was so caught up in a swift and just solution (plus they had royally hacked me off!) that I had lost all perspective.

I have recalled that conversation many times, especially about my answer to her question: "Why did you chase them?" "Because they ran!" How many times do teachers simply react to students rather than act purposefully? If a student can get a teacher to react angrily, he or she is the one in control. A student's hostility does not require us to feel likewise. There is absolutely nothing to be gained by getting angry, defensive, hostile, or outraged. Teachers must remind themselves, "I am the adult here. I am the boss of this room."

The older I get, the more I realize how much time I have wasted fighting insignificant battles. Now I save my energy for things that really count. When I am confronted with an insubordinate or arrogant student I ask myself, "What is my goal here? What can I do to best help this student resolve this situation? Is what I am about to do or say going to help foster the person I want this student to become?"

Sometimes I realize I am too caught up in the situation to be able to think clearly. Just as my principal taught me, I know that everything does not have to be solved at the moment it occurs. I can distance myself, calm down, think clearly, and address the situation on my terms, not the student's. I don't "run after" students anymore.

Stephen Covey talks about creating "win-win" situations. Believe me, without exception, any time a teacher confronts a student in front of the student's peers, it will never be "win-win." If the entire class is caught up as the audience in the dramatic power struggle between a teacher and a student, everybody loses.

Let's say that Jerry makes a hostile statement about another student. The teacher asks him to follow the class protocol and apologize. Jerry angrily says, "It wasn't my fault. She started it, and I am NOT going to apologize!"

The appropriate response would be to "move in" on Jerry and quietly say, "Jerry, I need for you to step out in the hall." Then back up and give him room to get out. If he refuses, stay still, remain very calm, and quietly say to another student, "Will you please go to the office and tell them I need help in getting Jerry to step out in the hall." Then ignore Jerry and calmly resume the lesson.

Jerry will probably stomp out of the room before help arrives, but even if he doesn't, remain dead calm! If Jerry does step out in the hall, wait for a stopping point, calmly give the other students something to do, then step out into the hall to talk with Jerry. Speak quietly, breathe deeply, move slowly, and do the things people do normally when they are feeling calm. This helps prevent an escalation to anger (emotions follow actions). Keep focusing on the long-term goals for the class as a whole, and Jerry in particular. If a teacher can do that, everybody wins.

It is also easier to remain calm when realizing that student behavior is seldom attributable to one cause. It usually involves the student's prior experience, his self-perception, his background, his relationships with others in the class, his relationship with his teacher(s), and any number of factors. Be very careful about attributing motive. Remember: students are seldom just out to get their teachers.

Teachers should apologize when they have misjudged a student, or overreacted in a situation. It is a great object lesson for students to see a teacher admit unfairness, or at least complicity, in the situation. The teacher who apologizes in the appropriate situation earns the respect and trust of students.

If teacher and student are too upset, de-escalate the situation by saying, "We are both too angry to deal with this now. Let's drop this for the time being and both think about it. Why don't we talk after class?"

If the situation involves a student who has become irrational, calmly say to her or him, "You are out of control right now. I'm going to give you a chance to rein yourself in before I call for assistance." One special education teacher I know tells students, "We can solve this right now or others will have to be involved." (She confided in me that this always works, and it's a good thing because she has no idea who "the others" would be. Evidently her students have an ominous view about who "they" are!)

Chapter 7 lists several activities that can be used to build classroom unity and trust. Students can be prepared ahead of time to use conflict resolution techniques. Some schools specifically train certain students to be mediators in difficult situations. It is much easier for teachers to stay calm if they are not the only one who is composed. Particularly distressing can be dealing with group disruptive behavior.

Here are some ideas for interventions when several students are involved in the disruption:

- Single out the most powerful offender and deal quietly with her or him.

- Have a heart-to-heart.

- Ask the students to write or draw their feelings and comments.

- Take a "time out."

- Do something outrageously silly and laugh.

- Invite others into the room (administrator, grandmother, custodian, older students).

Things to Consider Before Reacting to a Disruptive Student

- Could this be about your own need to "win"?

- Could you have misinterpreted the situation?

- Have you confronted the one who wasn't the primary instigator?

- Is the hostility which is directed towards you actually displaced aggression?

- Is the student just trying to get attention (even if it is negative)?
- Does the student feel that she or he is not being respected, or is losing face?
- Is it possible that this student really did misunderstand?
- Is this student acting out of a feeling of powerlessness or hopelessness?
- Could this student have been joking?
- Is this student just acting in a way that is typical of his age?

"Ms. Patton, I think you misinterpreted my message about staying calm in a crisis."

6. Be Consistently Fair

"Consistent" and "fair" may sound like the same thing, but they are not. In fact they can be mutually exclusive. A teacher can consistently expel children who chew gum. Is that fair? Adjust the discipline policy in consideration of two factors. First, each individual situation depending on the circumstances, and second, the knowledge of that particular student. Are these factors consistent? Which one should teachers favor? As much as possible, they should consider both.

Being consistent builds credibility with students. Giving the superintendent's daughter the same consequence given the disreputable troublemaker for the same infraction lets students know that the rules are for everyone. Enforcing a rule in the last ten minutes of the last period on the day before the Christmas holiday demonstrates that the teacher means what is said. Consistency with a stated policy helps teachers give comparable consequences for similar breaches without having to think about the decision each time. Teachers should be consistent, however, there is always the danger of becoming robotic and unfeeling when consistency is valued over fairness. My recommendation is that teachers always err to the side of fairness.

> *There is nothing so unjust as treating unequals as though they were equal.*

In his book *Self-Concept and School Achievement,* William Purkey talks about finding a disclaimer in a drag strip program that states, "Every effort is made to ensure that each entry has a reasonable chance of victory." Purkey believes that it would be a good idea for all schools to follow this maxim. I agree that the most fair thing we can do in school is make sure that ALL students feel that there is a reasonable chance for them to succeed! Otherwise, why should they try? Would you?

As a professional, a teacher should be able to recognize that some students do not have the same level of understanding, the same amount of self-control, nor the same history. Federal Public Law 94.142 stipulates that children identified with special needs cannot be punished for an action caused by their exceptionality (e.g., you cannot punish a child with Tourette's Syndrome for cursing in the classroom). Likewise, there are times that special circumstances for some students (special ed. or not) call for unique and creative solutions to individual behavior problems.

In all cases, make sure that the consequences are logical and reasonable for the behavior breach. A child caught chewing gum loses gum privileges. A child late to class is required to stay after class. Rather than just being punitive, it is helpful if the child actually learns something from the consequence. I like the idea of having her or him fill out a behavior journal or individual behavior plan to keep on file. When a situation is resolved, let it be over. Students should be able to start with a "clean slate" after a consequence has been carried out. On the following page is an example of a behavior explanation plan.

Behavior Explanation Plan

Student's Name _____

Class/Period _____ Date _____

I violated our class code by:

_____

_____

I chose to do this because:

_____

_____

A more appropriate choice would have been:

_____

_____

This is how I feel about what happened:

_____

_____

This is what I plan to do in the future to prevent a recurrence of my actions:

_____

_____

This is how my teacher can help me implement my plan:

_____

_____

           Date_____

Student's Signature _____

Teacher Comments:

_____

_____

_____

Drumming to the Beat of a Different Marcher
© 2003 by Incentive Publications, Inc., Nashville, TN

If the classroom policies are working for 24 out of 25 students, should the policies be changed? No. Meet in private with student #25 and work out an individual plan with her or him. My statement in such circumstances would be something like, "Stephanie, I see that this management plan is not working for you, so let's come up with something else just for you."

Remember that the teacher is in charge of the room. Each teacher knows better than anyone what will work for his or her students. Do not be afraid to make modifications when the situation calls for it.

On the next page is an individualized plan to use or modify as needed. The space for "other" to sign can be a friend, a staff member close to the child, a community member, or whoever else has the respect of the student.

Individual Behavior Plan

Student's Name _____

Class/Period _____ *Date* _____

Long-Range Goals for Student:

_____

_____

_____

Short-Term Target Goal:

_____

_____

_____

What Student Will Do to Meet Target Goal:

_____

_____

_____

What Teacher Will Do to Help Student Meet Target Goal:

_____

_____

_____

What Parent or Other Will Do to Help Student Meet Target Goal (optional):

_____

_____

_____

Drumming to the Beat of a Different Marcher

What will happen if student fails to meet target goal:

1st Time-

_____

_____

2nd Time-

_____

_____

Positive recognition student will receive for making target goal:

_____

_____

Positive recognition teacher will make for sustaining target goal by

_____ ____ *(insert time period).*

_____

_____

Date _____

Student's Signature ____ _____

Teacher's Signature _____

Parent or Other Signature (optional) _____

Comments and Dates:

_____

_____

_____

_____

_____

_____

Be prepared for other students to cry, "No fair! Why does she have different rules than we do?" My answer is, "I will always try to be fair, but that does not always mean I will be equal." I ask them, "If we all go to the doctor, does he give us all the same medicine? Why not?" "Can all people park in the blue zones? Why not?" Brainstorm with your students for other examples where fair does not mean equal.

As a teacher builds a reputation among students and parents for being egalitarian, they will question her or him less. It takes time to build a reputation. Be fair and be patient; it will happen.

Over the years most of my students have given me the benefit of the doubt most of the time. When they do question my decisions, I tell them, "I hope that you will trust me enough to believe that I am acting in good faith. You cannot know everything that I know about all the implications involved in this situation. I am the one in charge, and it is up to me to act in what I consider the best interest of all the parties. I will gladly hear your comments and suggestions, and I will make a decision based on the fairest way I know to resolve the issue." And then I do it. (Watch out Judge Judy, here I come!)

7. Be Caring

> *Our lives are shaped by those who love us [and] those who refuse to love us.*
> –John Powell

The more time you invest with students, and the more you know about them, the better a classroom manager you will be. It is important to know what turns a child on and what turns a child off. On the first or second day of class ask each of your students to fill out a sheet about themselves. (Use the one provided or create a new one.) I keep the sheets and periodically go back and read them before creating lessons or making important decisions about dealing with students.

Taking Inventory

Answer all parts of every question honestly and candidly. There are no right or wrong answers. All answers will be held in confidence.

1. What is your full name?

_____

_____

    What do you like to be called? _____

    Why? _____

_____

_____

2. List 10 words that describe you.

_____   _____

_____   _____

_____   _____

_____   _____

_____   _____

3. List the people that live in your home(s) and put 2 describing words after each name.

_____

_____

_____

_____

_____

_____

_____

_____

4. What do you think you will be like 5 years from now?

_____

_____

_____

5. Of all the things you do in your free time, which ones do you like best?

_____

_____

_____

6. Of all the things required of you in your life, which things do you like least?

_____

_____

_____

7. Who is your best friend? Why?

_____

_____

_____

8. What do you and your friends have in common?

_____

_____

_____

9. At what kinds of things do you excel?

_____

_____

_____

Drumming to the Beat of a Different Marcher
© 2003 by Incentive Publications, Inc., Nashville, TN

10. At school, what are your favorite things to do?

_____

_____

_____

11. At school, what are your least favorite things to do?

_____

_____

_____

12. What is your favorite book or movie? Why?

_____

_____

_____

13. If you could change this school, what changes would you make?

_____

_____

_____

14. If you were the teacher in this class, what five rules would you have?

_____

_____

_____

15. What is your major goal (ambition, dream) right now?

_____

_____

_____

16. Who is the person you admire the most? Why?

_____

_____

_____

17. What are you most afraid of?

_____

_____

_____

18. What is it about you that makes your friends like you?

_____

_____

_____

19. What is something I (the teacher) need to know about you?

_____

_____

_____

20. Write your own question and answer it.

_____

_____

_____

_____

_____

_____

_____

_____

Sometimes teachers make insensitive decisions based not on unkindness but on inadequate information. Teachers should find out all they can about the lives they touch daily. Drive through the district where students live. Note the exteriors of the homes, the vehicles parked around, and the general "feel" of the neighborhood. Make every effort to understand the students' culture. Watch what they watch on TV. Listen to their music. Talk to them. Find out the amount of time each child spends on the bus each day. What time do they have to get up to catch the bus? What time do they get home in the afternoon?

Knowing these things can help a teacher make more appropriate homework assignments, affect comments, and guide expectations. It is important to balance an understanding of the students' problems with clear statements of acceptable behavior choices. Students do not need for teachers to pity them, but they do need for teachers to understand them. Having an informed view of their lives bolsters a teacher's commitment to keep expectations high but reasonable.

The Issue of Discipline

Teachers are often told that in these days of paranoia and unrestricted litigation, it is best to never touch a child for any reason. I just cannot and will not support that notion. Some children are starved for appropriate human touch. I believe that teachers who feel comfortable hugging, patting, and otherwise affirming children should do it! Of course, be cautious if the situation warrants it (Be aware of the community norms and situations that are questionable. When in doubt, talk with a respected administrator or colleague.) Respect the student's limits; some students do not want to be touched at all. (They may have been harmed and are distrustful of adults.) Never touch a student in anger or to restrain her or him unless there is a safety issue. Keep physical contact—as well all things in the classroom—consistent with the long-term goals. When used wisely, the human touch is a powerful complement to caring. Above all, maintain the child's dignity.

8. Be Contemplative

Being contemplative means that teachers should spend much time and energy thinking about how to improve their techniques and strategies. Expert teachers did not become experts overnight. They tried new things, made mistakes, had successes, had failures, reflected on the results, decided what to keep and what to toss, and repeated the process over and over again. It's a little like mastery learning. You get one part right, and then you build on it. They key is for teachers to be constantly thinking about what they are doing and why they are doing it. Read, study, and think deeply about how it all fits together.

Whether a novice or an experienced educator, a classroom will run better in direct proportion to the amount of time spent planning, preparing, and reflecting.

Contemplative Teachers:

1. Plan how they will react to different situations.

2. Plan how they will reinforce positive behavior.

3. Plan how they will extinguish negative behavior.

4. Plan how they will individualize discipline practices for difficult students.

5. Plan how they will engage all learners.

6. Plan how they will differentiate instruction for diverse learners.

7. Plan how they will foster a classroom community.

8. Plan how they will build their own resiliency so that they will be at their personal best.

Planning principles five and six are discussed throughout Part 2 of this book. Keep in mind that they are integral parts of a management plan. Discipline works best when associated with good instructional/assessment methods. Rules, consequences, and rewards cannot be isolated from everything else that goes on in a classroom—it all works together. Discipline problems will be kept to a minimum when students are actively engaged and given the chance to feel successful in their work.

Helping students be successful means doing something meaningful and productive, not just making sure they achieve a certain score or grade. As teachers learn more about their subject areas and the culture of their students, they become more adept at utilizing good instructional techniques to help avert discipline problems.

Today more than ever, educators must focus not only on cognitive issues but also on the emotional literacy component of learning and working together (or what we Baby Boomers used to call the "affective domain," and some naysayers still call "that touchy-feely-I-need-to-validate-my-feelings stuff").

The eighth maxim simply says, the better you take care of yourself, the better you can take care of others. Period.

Effective teachers spend hours in preparation and contemplation. They learn from their mistakes, continue to consider ideas, try new things, and constantly ask themselves, "Is this working?" "Will this foster in students what I believe they need for lifetime goals?" Schools are not isolated entities. Forces outside the school shape the way things go inside the school. Become familiar with what those forces are and change the things you can change. Accept the things you cannot change, and do your best to work around them. Remember that some students may need more than any teacher can give. Involve others when necessary. Do what is possible and always leave the door open.

9. Be Courageous

I often tell new teachers to "Remember always: YOU ARE THE BOSS OF YOUR ROOM!" No one should tell a teacher otherwise. In the end it is the teacher who is accountable for everything that goes on in that classroom. Each teacher has every right to say what is acceptable and what is unacceptable in his or her own classroom.

Teachers do *not* have the right to say to students, "That kind of language is gutter filth! You are going to go straight to Hell if you continue to talk like that!" But they do have the right to say, "That kind of language is not appropriate for this classroom. Don't use it in here."

Teachers have a responsibility to demand respect for themselves and for all the students! Teachers also must maintain a safe and secure environment for themselves as well as for their students. Do whatever it takes to achieve these conditions.

Sometimes a teacher may be criticized by colleagues for not "going along with everybody else", or for "making the rest look bad." Parents may tell you, "Well, that's not the way Mr. Socrates did it!" (or "You are obviously unaware that our brother-in-law is on the school board!") It takes courage to march against the ranks, but if it is right for kids, do it!

Never forget that schools are first and foremost for the students!

In all cases teachers must be an advocate for children. So many kids today do not have a voice. Many are abused, afraid, ignored, angry, hurting, confused, and or at risk in some way. Teachers must speak out for their best interests.

Recommended Reading List

Burke, Kay. *What To Do with the Kid Who . . .* Arlington Heights, IL: Skylight Professional Development, 2000.

Canter, Lee, and Marlene Canter. *Lee Canter's Assertive Discipline: Positive Behavior Management for Today's Classroom.* Santa Monica: Lee Canter & Associates, 1992.

Canfield, Jack, and Howard Clive Wells. *100 Ways to Enhance Self-Concepts in the Classroom.* Englewood Cliffs, N.J.: Prentice-Hall, 1976.

Curwin, Richard L., and Allen N. Mendler. *Discipline with Dignity.* Alexandria, VA: Association for Supervised Curriculum (ASCD), 1988.

Glasser, William. *Control Theory in the Classroom.* NY: Harper & Row, 1986.

Glasser, William. *The Quality School: Managing Students without Coercion.* NY: HarperCollins, 1992.

Kohn, Alfie. *Beyond Discipline: From Compliance to Community.* Alexandria, VA: ASCD, 1996.

Kohn, Alfie. *Punished by Rewards: The Trouble with Gold Stars, Incentive Plans, A's, Praise, and Other Bribes.* Boston: Houghton Mifflin, 1993.

CHAPTER 2

Parental Involvement

If It Weren't for the Parents, We Wouldn't Have All These Kids in the First Place!

"So what's all this nonsense about
our daughter Shangrila violating a dress code?"

There was a time in American education when schools could count on parents for almost total support. Most students came from two-parent homes where schools were regarded as sacrosanct. Today's parents, on the other hand, may be single mothers, single fathers, stepmothers, stepfathers, grandmothers, "significant others," newly arrived immigrants, affluent, middle class, or impoverished. I was quite shocked the first time I realized that some of the parents of my students were little more than children themselves! The term "parent" can be used broadly to include the wide range of important adults in a child's life. In this chapter the term is referring to the primary care giver or person most responsible for the child's well-being, education, and development.

The issue of how important it is to involve our students' parents goes back to the guiding principle teachers must use for everything in education. What is the best way to ensure that both the short-term and long-range goals for students are met? In all cases, educators are better able to meet the needs of students if they have parents on their side. Therefore, teachers have to do everything possible to engage the parents as active participants in their children's education.

The National PTA

In their National Standards for Parent/Family Involvement Programs the National Parent Teacher Association (1997) cites research that clearly indicates:

1. When parents are involved, students achieve more, regardless of socioeconomic status, ethnic/racial background, or the parents' education level.

2. The more extensive the parent involvement, the higher the student achievement.

3. When parents are involved, students exhibit more positive attitudes and behavior.

4. Children from diverse cultural backgrounds tend to do better when

parents and professionals collaborate to bridge the gap between the culture at home and the learning institution.

5. Secondary students whose parents remain involved make better transitions, maintain the quality of their work, and develop realistic plans for their future. Students whose parents are not involved are more likely to drop out.

6. The most accurate predictor of a student's achievement in school is not income or social status, but the extent to which that student's family is able to:

   a) create a home environment that encourages learning

   b) communicate high, yet reasonable expectations for their children's achievement and future careers

   c) become involved in their children's education at school and in the community

Even though research has overwhelmingly demonstrated that the greatest predictor in a child's success in school is associated with the home factor, many teachers are hesitant to reach out to parents. They are sometimes stymied by the implied "Myth of the Good Teacher," which is the belief that really talented teachers never have to ask for help; teachers who truly do their jobs well require no other adult assistance for a smooth-functioning classroom.

That notion is as absurd as it is harmful. Teachers have a right to have parental support, but also a responsibility to ask for and expect it. No matter how talented a teacher is, he or she cannot provide the extended one-on-one time that parents can with their child.

Parental approval is a powerful motivator for students. A lack of participation on the part of the parent sends a message to the child that he or she is not worth the effort. An involved parent can provide the directed practice a child needs for mastering certain skills and the encouragement she or he needs for a lifetime of success. Never forget that parents are the most important, influential people in a child's life. Teachers cannot do their jobs effectively without them.

> *The best inheritance parents can give their children is a few minutes of their time each day.*
> – author unknown

There are effective techniques you, as an individual, can employ to involve the parents of the students you teach. The key terms for you to remember are *communicate, problem solve,* and *enlist support.*

Communicate

Beginning Communications With Parents

- Start early. Before school starts, or on the first day of school, make contact with the parents. Introduce yourself with a letter, and let them know that you want to work with them to help their child have the best year possible. Be friendly, be professional, be inviting, and be sure you use correct grammar and punctuation on all written communications! (I promise you that if you don't, some smart aleck will correct it in red and send it back to you!) You may want to use a fun font or clip art to make your letter seem less officious. Give them your contact information, and invite them to use it.

- Give the parents enough of an overview of your plans and expectations that they can see you know what you are doing.

- Provide a translation for parents who have limited use of English.

- Let them know how important they are in the ultimate success of their children's lives. Always demonstrate respect for the family and the family's primary role in helping students become responsible adults.

- Make the first move. Do not wait for parent to contact you. If you care about what happens to your students, you have to involve yourself with their parents.

- Make your first contact a positive one!

Top 10 Ways to Keep in Touch With Parents

- Phone
- Email
- Voice mail
- Fax
- Web site (school or class)
- Personal contacts
- Newsletters
- Academic calendar
- News bulletins/community bulletin boards
- Notes and cards (If all else fails, send parents a registered letter.)

Problem Solve

> *Anyone who says, "easy as taking candy from a baby" has never tried it!*
> – author unknown

In every communication teachers have with parents, the ultimate goal is to help the student. Teachers who are at cross-purposes with parents cannot help students. If there were one piece of advice I could give to teachers about dealing with parents it would be to treat parents as the teacher would wish to be treated. That sounds really simple, but sometimes parents make it difficult to be that compassionate. Once in a while, after an unpleasant encounter with parents it may appear that the student would fare much better as an orphan. However, never underestimate the power of parents!

Dealing with parents can tax a teacher's best interpersonal communication skills. Even expert classroom teachers often shy away from encounters with parents. It may be helpful for teachers to practice role-playing with a group of colleagues. Ask an administrator if a couple of faculty meetings could be devoted to having teachers practice their parent-conferencing skills. Experienced teachers can be a big help in supplying neophytes with strategies and phrases that will help them remain compassionate and in control.

Tips on Problem Solving With Parents

Keep parents up-to-date on what is going on with their child. If grades or behavior take a downward plunge, let the parents know immediately. Parents do not like surprises! An often-repeated question parents ask is, "Why didn't I know about this sooner?" Indeed, why didn't they? There is little defense for not alerting parents to potential problems. There is often a good chance they can help prevent the bigger problem.

Do communicate what is happening in the classroom. Whether it is changing the discipline plan, initiating a new test policy, or planning a field trip, parents want to know what is going on. Tell them. Do not be defensive! Let parents know that their child's teacher is in charge and capable. Explain policies and procedures, but do NOT apologize for them.

Do not attempt to solve problems at chance encounters with a parent or guardian. The grocery store check-out line, the school football game, or the church parking lot are not locations conducive to a professional meeting. Have the parents come to school at a time you can give them your full attention and have ready access to your grade book and the student's work.

Establish a common ground with parents. Both teacher and parent are there to act in the best interest of a child. Even if a teacher and the parents have to "agree to disagree" on an issue, find commonality in the commitment to the student's welfare.

Expect parents' full support. Speak to parents as equals in the problem-solving process. If they come to school to talk, sit beside them in adult chairs. Do not apologize for bothering them at home or at work. When acting on their child's behalf, no apology is needed.

Help parents identify the specifics of the problem. Show them documentation whenever possible. Make notes as they supply information or ask questions. Write down the plan of action agreed to and give them a copy.

Give parents very concrete, specific ways to help. Some of their most important contributions can be very simple—turning off the TV (also CD players, computer games, and cell phones), instituting a quiet study time, making sure the child has a place to work, and asking them to look at completed assignments.

Try to say to the parents early in the conversation, "But I'm sure I'm not telling you anything that you don't already know." I nod my head while saying, "I'm sure you see the same behavior at home, right?" Before they know it, they are nodding right along with me and admitting that the problem is not unique to my classroom.

Ask for and listen to parents' advice about how to handle situations with their child(ren). Questions such as "How do you deal with it?" and "What is working for you?" help parents to think about solving the problem rather than defending the behavior.

Be empathetic and compassionate, but stick to the subject. Don't let the parent wander off into areas that have no solution or no relevance. Avoid blaming. Gather as much information as possible.

Provide a follow-up plan to check on progress. End the meeting by recapping the important points and setting a time to be back in touch.

Be alert to common excuses and ploys:

"Oh, none of us Johnsons has ever been very good at math." That's either a rationalization for not dealing with the inadequacy or guilt for not having addressed it earlier. Accept their explanation non-judgmentally, but keep moving them toward a solution.

"She doesn't listen to anything I say. I tell her to turn off the TV and study, but she won't."

Bolster the parent's responsibility and inevitable accountability. Offer to bring in outside resources. Give positive suggestions and hold your ground!

Occasionally a teacher will encounter a parent that gives the teacher carte blanche privileges to discipline his or her child. Rather than seeing this as supportive, acknowledge it for what it is: an abdication of the parent's obligation to help the child extinguish inappropriate behaviors. They are asking the teacher to act in their stead rather than deal with the unpleasant task of enforcing rules and following up with consequences.

Understand that some problems are simply too overwhelming or too disturbing for parents. Assure them that even serious problems have solutions. Suggest other experts to help deal with the problem.

Remember that educators are required by law to report incidences of child abuse. Period. It is not only a moral issue, but also a legal one. A teacher who is suspicious (but not sure) should consult a counselor or an administrator. Carefully document all suspected occurrences.

Finally, when communicating with parents, do not use jargon and definitely try to keep your sense of humor!

Too Much Parental Support

Parental support isn't just about baking cookies or chaperoning the class party anymore. Some parents are asking to be more and more involved in decisions dealing with curriculum, schedules, school policies, and virtually all aspects of the educational community. Sometimes there is a fine line between supporting the school's purpose and getting in the way of it. Usually when I am invited to do a workshop on parental involvement it is in response to low or nonexistent parental support in a school or district. However, there are occasions when teachers and administrators have the opposite problem. They feel that their parents are too involved and/or overpowering. There are some situations where a parent seems to have become a "Professional Michael's Mom," or a litigious "Anna Advocate."

I have heard some educators say that they would rather have parents be totally inattentive than for them to be "over-involved" with their children's education. I disagree. I find that it is easier to divert excessive attention than it is to generate it when there is little or none to begin with. At least the disproportionately attentive parent is interested in his or her child's welfare.

If dealing with a parent who is usurping a teacher's authority or becoming over-involved in classroom operations, try the following tips:

Dealing With An Over–Involved Parent

1. Be proactive. Invite their involvement when it is convenient for the teacher.

2. Ask the parent to volunteer in classes or areas other than those his or her child attends.

3. Dilute their power by asking under-represented groups to serve on committees, chair events, and volunteer with them.

4. Steer them towards working for the benefit of all students, and sincerely praise their efforts. (Many times these folks are just starved for attention or for the chance to contribute something meaningful.)

5. Clearly identify their limits. Let them know the teacher is in charge and has ultimate veto power.

6. Be cautious about sharing information regarding other students, faculty, or administrators. Non-school personnel should not be privy to any confidential information. Gossip is a huge (and extremely unprofessional) no-no!

7. Keep a sense of self; do not be caught up in parent agendas.

8. Invite them to help get other parents involved.

9. Remind them that it is natural to want a child to *do* his or her best, but it is unfair and unrealistic to ask her or him to *be* the best.

10. Always maintain a sense of humor. (Sooner or later his or her child will move on, and so will he or she.)

Some members of our profession lament, "It's not my job to teach these parents how to be parents! It's all I can do to teach their children!" I realize that teachers are asked to assume far too many duties and responsibilities as it is. However, I often ask myself and my colleagues, "If we don't do it, who will?"

Occasionally, a parent just needs a listening ear or the reassurance that the child's behavior is a normal developmental stage and will soon pass. Sometimes I can give them the gift of pointing out strengths in their child they had not before recognized (most of them associated with Gardner's 8 Levels of Intelligence).

> *The potential of a child*
> *is the most intriguing thing*
> *in all creation.*
> – Ray Lyman Wilbur

I have encountered family problems that are far beyond the scope of my expertise or training. In those cases, I am quick to refer parents to more qualified professionals. However, I find that many parents are simply asking my advice on how they can be better parents. I have several favorite resources.

One source I have is a collection of information sheets for parents published by the National Association of Elementary School Principals (NAESP). Their members receive a regular supplement (written both in English and Spanish) called "Report to Parents." Educators are invited to include the reports with their school newsletters to parents. NAESP gives full permission for the pages to be reproduced. Current topics such as bullying, over-scheduling children, child safety, children and drugs, antidotes for violence, TV watching, and other timely topics are covered in a simple, applicable style. These supplements make excellent starting points for teacher-parent communications.

For parents who are particularly negative or critical of their children, I ask them to fill out the following sheet.

What I See In My Child

Put your child's name in the center square. Fill in the spaces around his or her name with words that describe the strengths you see in her or him. Place the most important attributes in the spaces closest to the center. You can use words from the Strength Word List on the following page, or use your own. When you have filled in all the spaces, give this sheet to your child.

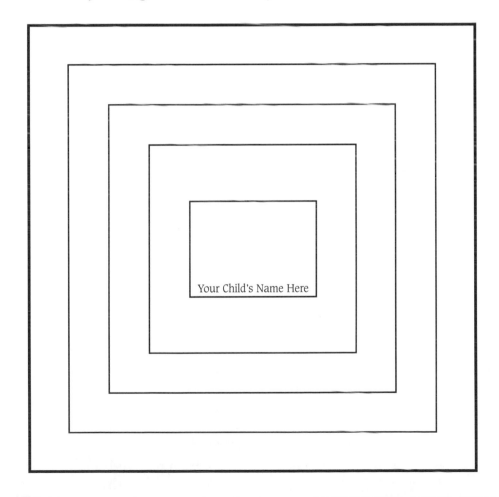

Your Child's Name Here

Strength Word List
(These can help you get started.)

Be sure to include words that describe your child's:

SPIRITUAL STRENGTHS	MENTAL STRENGTHS	PHYSICAL STRENGTHS	EMOTIONAL STRENGTHS
romantic	investing	serene	prudent
busy	strong-willed	organizer	confident
kind	motivated	tactful	tireless
artistic	understanding	committed	industrious
careful	disciplined	spontaneous	thoughtful
convincing	self-reliant	commanding	expressive
friendly	persistent	tolerant	settled
gentle	neat	goal-directed	persuasive
loyal	caring	progressive	affectionate
distinctive	thinker	sharp	graceful
perfectionist	clever	capable	reliable
exact	self-determined	certain	leader
tenacious	well-informed	looked up to	growing
balanced	creative	dedicated	eager
ambitious	orderly	courageous	active
outgoing	individualistic	consistent	influential
steadfast	searching	honorable	giving
poised	appreciative	productive	original
strong	fair-minded	determined	thrifty
considerate	respected	planner	unselfish
fulfilled	flexible	efficient	self-aware
manager	likes new ideas	cooperative	self-directed
open-minded	forceful	dependable	adjusted
talented	predictable	comforting	inquiring
witty	intelligent	sociable	practical
systematic	encouraging	serious	unique
trustworthy	imaginative	adaptable	precise
foresight	pursuing	forgiving	listener
empathetic	compassionate	visionary	humorous
cheerful	motivating	artistic	athletic
energetic	disciplined	sharing	caring
daring	risk taker	courageous	patient
coordinated	loyal	fun-loving	perceptive

Drumming to the Beat of a Different Marcher

For parents who are having a tough time communicating with their children, I give them this tip sheet:

Helpful Hints for Communicating with Your Child

1. Listen with your FULL attention. A good way to ensure their full attention is put them in the front seat of your car and drive them around as you talk with them. (Unless they want to hurl themselves from a moving vehicle, they've got no place to run.)

2. Be aware of body language, both yours and theirs.

3. Use silence to understand your child's meanings and feelings.

4. Use open responses to keep the child talking. "I see." "Tell me more about that part."

5. Accept and respect your child's feelings. Feelings don't have to be justified, they just ARE.

6. Don't interrupt.

7. Check out your child's feelings by reflecting what she or he says: "I think I heard you say that you were really angry with Susan." "So you were feeling helpless? Like you wanted to hide?"

8. Be calm. Speak in a quiet voice. Use economy of words (don't talk too much).

9. Stick to the subject.

10. Don't assume that you are making yourself clear. Check for understanding periodically. "Can you tell me in your own words what you think I'm telling you?"

11. Problem solve by discussing a variety of solutions. Emphasize your child's choice in selecting a plan of action.

12. Give your point of view as just that. It's not the law or the only good solution.

13. Don't be a dictator. Remember that children also learn by failing. Once in a while, allow the child to learn successful problem solving by failing.

14. Avoid nagging, threatening, criticizing, lecturing, or probing.

15. NO name-calling! Attack the problem, not the person.

16. Whenever possible, use humor.

All educators need to do a better job of speaking up for themselves and promoting the educational system they represent. Teaching children does not happen in a vacuum. So much of what goes on in class is a reflection of what goes on in the community, it is ridiculous to try and separate the two. Building an alliance with parents and the rest of the community is one of the best practices educators have for ensuring that both short-term and long-range educational goals for children are met.

To open the lines of communication between parents and their children, I administer the following tests. I ask that they go to different rooms or to different areas of the same room to answer the following questionnaire.

For the Parent to Take About His or Her Child:

How Much Do You Know About Your Child?

1. If your child had a choice, what would he or she prefer to be called? _____

2. Who is your child's closest friend? _____

3. Who does your child most admire? _____

4. Of what is your child most afraid? _____

5. What is your child's favorite thing to do with his or her friends?

_____

6. What is your child's favorite kind of music? _____

7. What was the best movie your child ever watched?

_____

8. At what age does your child plan to leave home? _____

9. What is your child's favorite color? _____

10. If your child had to wear one outfit for a month, which outfit would it be? _____

11. What most embarrasses your child?

_____

Drumming to the Beat of a Different Marcher
©2003 by Incentive Publications, Inc., Nashville, TN

12. If your child could change one thing about herself/himself, what would it be?

_____

13. If your child could change one thing about your family, what would it be?

_____

14. What trait do you have that your child most values?

_____

15. What trait do you have that your child would most like to change?

_____

16. If there were suddenly no electricity in the world, what appliance would your child miss the most? _____

17. What is your child's weight (within 2 pounds)? _____

18. What was your child's proudest moment?

_____

_____

19. What was your child's saddest moment?

_____

_____

20. If your child could make one wish come true, what would it be?

_____

_____

TOTAL _____

Compare your answers with those of your child. Score one point for each answer that is the same or reasonably close. If you score **16 or better**, congratulate yourself for really knowing your child. If your score is **11–15**, you may want to think about spending more time catching up with what is new with your child. If your score is **10 or less**, you definitely need to spend more time finding out about what is going on with your child.

About You:

1. If you had a choice, what would you prefer to be called?

_____

2. Who is your closest friend?_____

3. Who do you most admire? _____

4. Of what are you most afraid?_____

_____

5. What is your favorite thing to do with your friends?

_____

6. What is your favorite kind of music? _____

_____

7. What was the best movie you ever watched?

_____

8. At what age do you plan to leave home?_____

9. What is your favorite color? _____

10. If you had to wear one outfit for a month, which outfit would it be?

_____

11. What most embarrasses you? _____

_____

12. If you could change one thing about yourself, what would it be?

_____

13. If you could change one thing about your family, what would it be?

_____

14. What trait do you have that you most value?

_____

15. What trait does your parent have that you would most like to change?

_____

16. If there were suddenly no electricity in the world, what appliance would you miss the most? _____

17. What is your weight (within 2 pounds)? _____

18. What was your proudest moment?

_____

_____

_____

19. What was your saddest moment?

_____

_____

_____

20. If you could make one wish come true, what would it be?

_____

_____

_____

_____

Now compare your answers to those of your parent. Give her/him one point for every answer that is the same or reasonably close (you be the judge). Your parent has the scoring code.

Recommended Reading List for Educators

Beckwith, Harry. *Selling the Invisible: A Field Guide to Modern Marketing.* NY Warner Books, 1997.

Canter, Lee, and Patricia R. Sarka. *Parents on Your Side.* Santa Monica: Lee Canter & Associates, 1991.

McEwan, Elaine K. *How to Deal with Parents Who Are Angry, Afraid, Troubled or Just Plain Crazy.* Thousand Oaks, CA: Corwin Press, 1998.

Pelzer, David. *A Child Called "It:" One Child's Courage to Survive.* Deerfield Beach, FL: Health Communications, 1995.

Stepp, Laura Sessions. *Our Last Best Shot: Guiding Our Children through Early Adolescence.* NY: Riverhead Books, 2001.

Recommended Reading List for Parents

Covey, Sean. *7 Habits of Highly Effective Teens: The Ultimate Teenage Success Guide.* NY: Simon & Schuster, Inc., 1998.

Hallowell, Edward M., and John J. Ratey. *Driven To Distraction. Recognizing and Coping with Attention Deficit Disorder from Childhood through Adulthood.* NY: Simon & Schuster, 1994.

Shedd, Charlie W. *You Can Be a Great Parent!* Waco: Word Books, 1970.

Salt, J.S. *Always Kiss Me Good Night. Instructions on Raising the Perfect Parent.* NY: Three Rivers Press, 1997.

Shapiro, Lawrence E. *How to Raise a Child with a High E.Q: A Parent's Guide to Emotional Intelligence.* NY: HarperCollins Publishers, Inc., 1997.

Different Beats
(Differentiating Instruction)

The second part of this book deals with ideas and techniques connected to instruction and assessment. Movement between the two should be natural, additive, and seamless. Through both varied instructional methods and diverse assessment strategies students can acquire and demonstrate deep understandings about a common core of knowledge.

All students learn; it is important to recognize that they learn at different rates and in different ways. The teacher's job is to capitalize on a student's natural strengths to help them find their own best means for learning.

In Chapter 3, The Learning Cycle, a promising constructivist approach is outlined. In a learning cycle lesson students are asked to develop their own understandings through exploration, investigation, and participation. Carefully guided questioning and application yields knowledge that is extremely personal and meaningful. Lesson plans for all grade levels and disciplines are enhanced by the use of this model.

Chapter 4 focuses on newly evolving brain research about Multiple Intelligences, learning styles, and flow state. Ways to maximize student strengths, to help them compensate for areas where they are not so strong, are emphasized. Differentiated instruction and assessment are identified as ways of ensuring that all students have a reasonable chance at success.

Chapter 5 is about cooperative learning. The use of small group interactions in learning situations can lead to Higher-Order thinking, enhanced feelings of individual self-esteem, and greater academic achievement. Cooperative learning is an effective instructional and assessment strategy that can improve student learning and promote emotional literacy among peers.

Chapter 6 discusses advances in technology and how it can be put to effective use in the classroom. Benefits and drawbacks of using technology are considered, and a list of popular educational web sites is provided.

PART 2
Different Beats (Differentiating Instruction)

CHAPTER 3

The Learning Cycle

Training Wheels
for Your Learning Cycle

Most educators have spent hours in teacher preparation programs learning how to write lesson plans. Therefore, they are usually very familiar with how to create behavioral objectives that will meet stated goals. In teaching my methods courses at the university, I require my pre-service students to do the same thing, but with one twist: I require that they write every lesson plan using a constructivist model, the learning cycle. The reason I have them use this model is because I believe that students have more success and more positive attitudes about school when they share responsibility for their own learning.

Queen of the Teeter–Totter

By Debbie Silver

Melissa's in the upper group,
A verified class leader.
Little Julie sits in back,
A proven low non-reader.

The teacher has them open texts
To read about a lever.
She tells them they must learn the facts
To be a high achiever.

Melissa does her worksheet fast,
She writes each definition.
But Julie mixes up the words,
And gives up in submission.

"Poor Julie," says the teacher then,
"You cannot do this science.
With our state's standards as they are,
You'll never make compliance!"

Drumming to the Beat of a Different Marcher

She sighs and sends the kids to play
Melissa leads them proudly,
"I made the best grade in the class,"
She tells the others loudly.

But on the playground Julie reigns
She rules the teeter-totter.
She strands Melissa in mid-air
And knows just how she got her!

On Julie's chart the teacher writes
"She's such a slow responder.
She'll never learn how fulcrums work,
The concept's just beyond her!"

> *"The single most important factor influencing learning is what the learner already knows."*
> – David Ausubel

If it's so evident that this is not the best way for students to learn, why don't all teachers change their methods? For some it is extremely difficult to break with a tradition that is so deeply ingrained in the institution of school. The industrialized version of what education should be is firmly grounded in the R3 method—read, recite, and regurgitate. This style is expedient, easily replicated, and most effortlessly assessed. Designers of this methodology purposefully avoided having a system that required teachers to be creative, intuitive problem solvers. Their belief is that instructors cannot be trusted to make decisions based on the individual needs of children. They want a curriculum that is "teacher proof," and in the process they have fostered a league of educators who are "student proof."

The reality is that teachers live in a standards-based world in which accountability often means that students are required to demonstrate common literacy and skills acquisition. Inasmuch as students who enter school have different knowledge levels resulting from diverse experiences, backgrounds, and cultural values, teachers must take these factors into account and present new information in a meaningful way to each learner's existing knowledge. The task can seem daunting, but there is a relatively simple lesson design that has been used successfully by teachers across disciplines and for all grade levels to accomplish this end.

Teaching Those Who Hear a "Distant Drummer"

Teachers can use the instructional model called the Learning Cycle to help children make sense of their worlds. Instructors of all levels and all subjects can modify traditional lesson plans so that no student is left behind. When using the Learning Cycle, lessons begin with that which students already know. These lessons are intentionally designed to "level the playing field" so that all learners have a reasonable chance at success.

> **Imagination**
> *Raise new questions*
> *Explore new possibilities*
> *Regard old problems from a new angle.*
> – Albert Einstein

One of the concerns of traditional educators is that teaching "those who step to a different beat" will take away time and other resources better spent getting as many students as possible to pass standardized tests. Without going into an argument for the legitimacy of "teaching to a test," let me just say that assessing for true understanding has little to do with merely acquiring isolated facts of content knowledge.

More and more educators today are viewing "teaching" as an interactive verb that requires the engagement of the learner as well. A teacher may say it, write it, demonstrate it, or in any other manner make a sincere effort to convey it to students, but if the students do not learn it, it cannot be said that the teacher *taught* it. Thus, the focus today is shifting away from teachers being the gatekeepers of all knowledge and rules to one in which the teacher interacts with the curriculum and the students by planning interactive learning tasks, designing more authentic types of assessment, and redirecting time and energy (Vatterott, 1995).

What would happen if all teachers began to "drum to the beat of their different marchers" instead of forcing all students into the same paced teacher-centered instructional model? In a study conducted by a superintendent in 1990, school principals were assigned to shadow 45 students in 9 different settings. Among other things, they reported that most of the classes they observed were boring and not engaging. They found a disproportionate number of African-American and Hispanic students placed in special programs. They reported scant evidence that participation in programs for mildly handicapped students had benefit. Despite these findings, their school district was eventually able to improve overall test scores and morale by including more special education students in regular education classes and promoting a more constructivist curriculum for all students (Lytle, 1996).

Unless students can balance their experiential knowledge with newly presented information, they will not be able to learn it and use it. Piaget (1974) described this occurrence as "finding equilibration through accommodation and assimilation of new information." Effective teachers have always been able to engage their students by relating what was to be learned to what they already knew. They seem to have a sense of where their students are in their understandings, and armed with that knowledge, they virtually "go in after them." These educators realize that students can better construct new meanings by actively seeking to make sense of things on their own rather than having the lessons presented in an already established format. Instruction begins by purposefully addressing students' predisposed misconceptions.

In her 1999 book *The Differentiated Classroom: Responding to the Needs of All Learners,* Carol Ann Tomlinson concurs that a classroom that is healthy for learners is characterized by the fact that what is taught and learned:

- is relevant to students; it seems personal, familiar, and connected to the world they know
- helps students understand themselves and their lives more fully now and will continue to do so as they grow up
- is authentic, offering "real" history or math or art, not just exercises about the subject
- can be used immediately for something that matters to the student
- makes students more powerful in the present as well as the future

Same Content, Different Strategy

For educators who are discouraged by all the "latest and greatest" trends we have endured in education, let me assure you that I am not talking about an abandonment of all that has previously been taught. Actually, all that really needs to be done is to shift the responsibility of learning onto students rather than teachers trying to provide all the informational output.

Do you remember how textbooks used to be written? They started with a list of the new vocabulary words, a fact list, and an introduction of the topic. Next there were lots of examples and rules followed by skill development practice exercises. Then there was the objective end-of-the-chapter test. But at the very end of the chapter there were some really thought-provoking activities and discrepant events. They were called things like "For Enrichment" and "Going Further." Most of my teachers only let the early finishers attempt them. Looking back, I realize that if my teachers had started with those fun, challenging activities, I would have been much more likely to have responded to the rest of the lesson.

Luckily, many textbooks today are written from a Learning Cycle perspective. Often they start each new lesson with a discrepant event, an interesting link, or a thought-provoking question. However, teachers do not need to be slaves to textbook writers. Any core or encore curriculum can be adapted to meet the Learning Cycle model.

Why Discrepant Events?

As stated before, teaching is an active verb that requires the engagement of the learner. Because it has become harder and harder to capture the attention of students, discrepant events are a way to stimulate interest in a particular topic.

For instructional purposes, discrepant events can be described as an investigation in which the new information that is introduced is inconsistent with information previously thought to be true (misconceptions). Piaget referred to this type of learning when he described how learners can be motivated to learn if they experience a sense of "disequilibration." As long as the learner's environment is stable, mental activity is not necessary. But when an unfamiliar problem arises the learner must use prior experience, new insights, and/or peer interaction to solve the problem and reestablish equilibration. Equilibration can be restored through accommodation whereby the learner creates or restructures his or her thought patterns or through assimilation whereby the learner incorporates the new information into existing thought patterns.

A discrepant event can encompass all of the above. It arouses interest and allows for exploration, discovery, questioning, and discussion. This involvement and interaction between students and their environment will initiate linking and application. Discrepant events can be used to help students learn.

The Learning Cycle

Although it is generally enhanced by the use of cooperative learning, the Learning Cycle can be incorporated into most teaching situations with little modification of classroom arrangement or materials. It primarily involves an ideological shift in lesson presentation and teaching responsibility. The basic idea is to begin lessons by engaging students in hands-on exploration rather than giving them vocabulary lists, lectures, or lists of rules.

Using the Learning Cycle

In a science class: The teacher holds up a standard piece of typing paper and tries to "fly" it across the room. The student giggles as she or he unsuccessfully makes several attempts to get the paper to move in the direction he or she wants. She or he then distributes paper, scissors, and paper clips. Students are asked to do whatever they like to their papers in order to get them to travel the farthest distance across the room. The children design, fold, cut, compare, fly, modify, retry, discuss, and finally emerge with finished products ready for testing. During the exploration student comments range as follows:

"Hey, his is going farther than mine. I'm going to fold my wings like that!"

"Look, if you get rid of some of the extra paper, it will stay in the air longer."

"I'm making my wings pointed because I've never seen an airplane that wasn't pointed!"

The teacher is using the first stage of the learning cycle to engage students in solving a problem that requires them to use process skills to gather and organize data. She or he closely monitors the group and guides them through open-ended questions addressed to individuals and groups:

"Do you think there's a reason that airplanes have pointed noses? What could it be?"

"Why do you think folding the wings makes the plane go farther than leaving them flat?"

"Is there anything else that flies that is modeled like this?"

In this lesson, the teacher is using an exploratory activity that allows all students to encounter the same experience at the same time, giving them an equal starting point from which to construct their learning. By encouraging students to become active participants in their own learning, the teacher's role changes from "teller of facts" to "facili-

Drumming to the Beat of a Different Marcher

tator of discovery." In first asking students to use their prior knowledge to construct a product, she or he has engaged them in learning through an activity that arouses their interest and allows for exploration, discovery, questioning, and discussion (Silver, 1998).

As the students continue to explore, they discover that certain laws of aerodynamics seem to apply to all of their creations. They begin to articulate what they have observed in their own words. The teacher helps them translate such terms as "falls down" to "the pull of gravity" and "the harder you throw it" to "thrust." Next, he or she may show a computer model of flight along with appropriate dialogue to help develop the concepts and clarify the explanations. Because of their prior shared concrete experience, students are ready to participate in scientific discussions about lift, yaw, thrust, drag, and gravity. They are able to compare their observations from the data they collected in their previous explorations.

Once the students demonstrate an understanding of how actual flight occurs, the teacher asks them to apply what they have learned to pictures or computerized versions of cartoons involving flight. Learners are asked to state whether or not they believe the cartoon characters and contraptions could really fly and give rational explanations for their hypotheses. Students can be asked to circle the areas of discrepancy and indicate how they believe this might be remedied. The children are actively involved in learning as they use their newly acquired skills and understandings to construct deeper meanings and broader applications of their discoveries.

With this lesson, the teacher has guided the students through the three phases of the learning cycle (also called discovery learning):

- exploration
- concept development
- concept application

It should be noted that the learning cycle has been described in similar forms with steps of varying names whose numbers range from 3 to 6. For the purpose of this chapter, I have used a model first presented to me in 1987 at an NSF-sponsored Operations Physics Training Program in San Diego, CA. The model has its roots in the Science Curriculum Improvement Study (SCIS), an NSF-sponsored elementary science program developed in the 1960s. Regardless of the number and names of the steps in a particular model, the learning cycle is never a one-way progression. At any point in a lesson, learners may shift back and forth among the phases. It is the teacher's responsibility to monitor and informally assess where the students are, and where they need to go next.

The Learning Cycle's Three Phases

Exploration Phases
Concept Development Phase
Concept Application Phase

Exploration Phase

The exploration phase initiates students' interaction with information, materials, and each other in order to investigate an open-ended question. All class members are given common, concrete experiences that challenge them to gather and organize data and compare their answers. Lessons involving paradoxical or conflicting information capitalize on their natural curiosity.

Concept Development Phases

The concept development phase builds on student curiosity, discoveries, and inquiries as the teacher assimilates data that students have organized. Then it clarifies terms and concepts they have developed. In this phase, students are far more receptive to vocabulary lists, direct instruction, and investigating other resources because their earlier explorations have shown them the relevance of the lesson. They also are far more likely to retain ideas and concepts because they begin to see patterns and connections to their knowledge of the world.

Concept Application Phase

During the concept application phase the teacher challenges students to apply their knowledge to real-world situations and to explore broader applications of their discoveries. At this point, the teacher can pose new situations and questions to ensure deeper understanding.

In a math class: Students are asked to count the number of squares in the picture.

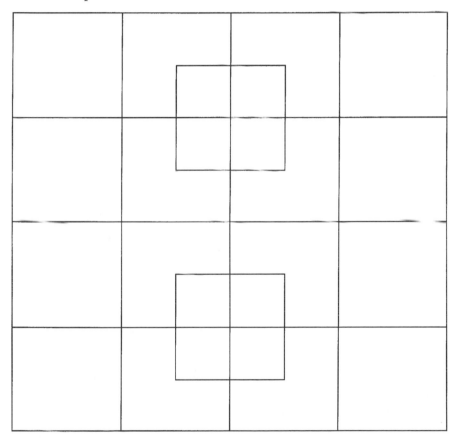

Answers vary from 27–40. The teacher looks at the class uncertainly, then places a transparency of the squares on the overhead projector and begins to count the obvious squares (the 1 big one, the 18 small ones, and the 8 tiny ones in the middle) and says, "See? There are just 27." Outraged students point out the teacher forgot to count squares formed by the 2 x 2 squares. The teacher agrees they are correct and counts 9 additional squares. "You are right! There are actually 36 squares." A few very observant students tell her that she has forgotten to count the 4 squares formed by the 3 x 3 small squares. "Well, I'll be. You are right again! There are 4 of those, and that makes 40 in all!"

The teacher then says, " When I asked you to count the squares, what were you looking for?" Some students say "Something that has 4 sides." The teacher draws a 4-sided object with curved lines. The students say, "No, the 4 sides have to be straight." The teacher draws a rectangle. The students say, "No, the 4 sides have to be straight and equal." The teacher draws a rhombus. The students again modify their definition to include a right angle. The teacher sums it up, "Okay, a square has to have 4 straight equal sides and a 90° angle, is that correct?" Because the students are the ones who generated the definition, they are far more likely to remember it.

For an assessment, the teacher passes out sheets with all kinds of polygons drawn on it. She asks the students to tell her whether or not each polygon is a square and tell her why. She then challenges students to create a piece of artwork using only squares.

In a language arts class: After students have mastered the concept of nouns, verbs, and adjectives, the teacher hands groups of students a copy of a story from a popular teen magazine. She asks students to compile a list of all the words ending in "ly." She tells them to group the "ly" words according to their functions in the sentences. Then she asks students to look for any emerging patterns they detect and be ready to report them to the whole group.

Students point out that most of their "ly" words are used to fine-tune other words, which are verbs, adjectives, and other words. The teacher then introduces the term "adverb" and asks the students if they can come up with a general rule about "ly" words. They tell her that words ending in "ly" are adverbs.

She writes the following phrases on the board:

she sang brilliantly

he cried long and hard

a lovely flower

she wants it done now

their progress was painstakingly slow

a scholarly report

driving exceedingly fast

he surely knew the answer

a truly beautiful sunset

a tiny fly

Students are asked to test their hypothesis about all "ly" words being adverbs. Through thoughtful, probing questions, the teacher helps students discover that not all words ending in "ly" are adverbs, and words which act as adverbs do not all end in "ly."

The teacher then asks students to create a poem, a song, a rap, an advertisement, or a short paragraph that contains at least 15 adverbs used correctly.

In a social studies class: The teacher gives each group of students a fictitious land map. The map key helps students locate water sources, mountains, fertile soil, desert areas, trees, caves, and natural resources. It shows average temperature and rainfall for each region. Each group is to pretend that they are early settlers and decide where they will establish their town. A representative from each group presents their group's location plans and tells why they selected it.

The teacher then guides the students in finding similar selections and reasons among all groups. Together the teacher and students decide which locations would make the best choices. The teacher then gives students a map of the towns actually established by early settlers moving west. They compare the early town locations with the criteria established in their introductory activity. Students read in their history books about the westward movement.

For an assessment, students are asked to pick any major city in the United States and discuss what factors initially contributed to its location.

Why the Learning Cycle Works

Instructional specialists advocate this kind of student-centered, active learning because it gives learners tasks that relate to their concerns, allows them to pursue their own interests, offers links to the outside world, and stimulates curiosity by introducing unexpected or unique information.

Learning is dependent on these factors:

1. The student's motivation.

2. The student's active involvement in the experience of learning.

3. Linking the new concepts with familiar information.

4. Being able to take new information and apply it to the real world.

Exploration

Often the exploration phase of the learning cycle is launched with a situation or question designed to capture the interest of students. A problem can be posed in which new information that is introduced is inconsistent with knowledge previously thought to be true (i.e. the teacher cannot just fly a flat piece of paper across the room). During this motivational phase students are encouraged to manipulate materials and explore ideas without the specific outcomes designated by the teacher. Students use their skills to gather and organize data.

Most learning cycle advocates suggest that teachers use classroom activities to make sure that all students share the same experience. Students who have not achieved proficiency in English, who are mainstreamed into classes, or who have not had the same experiential background as their peers can find themselves at a disadvantage for learning in a traditional setting; the exploration phase helps build a common ground for all. Some subjects more easily lend themselves to active classroom activities than others, but no matter what the subject, it is imperative that the lesson starts from a point shared by all.

Many teachers find that they can use a collective past experience (being scared at night, visiting a relative, eating a favorite food, solving a mystery) to illustrate a concept or begin a discussion. My advice regarding drawing on common experiences is to be sure that they are indeed shared by each student.

In the early 70s I was teaching middle grades students in an extremely rural community. We were all delighted when the first "local" mall was built in the closest big city, which was about a 50-minute drive away. Several months after the mall had opened, I decided to include a remembered trip to the mall to create a little enthusiasm for a writing assignment. I asked my students to raise their hands if they had visited the mall. All hands went up.

I put the students into groups and asked them to come up with a list of descriptive words to describe their mall experience. The activity was a major flop. Irritable students snapped at each other, disagreed, and generally botched the assignment. I did not know why.

That spring I figured it out when we took our students to the city on a field trip. We had extra time, so we made a stop at the mall on the way home. A group of girls followed me into a large department store, and as we were standing there getting our bearings, one of the young ladies nudged me and asked, "Ms. Silver, how much does it cost to ride the ride?" I had no idea what she was talking about. "What ride?" I asked. She pointed to the escalator. Then it dawned on me—she had never in her life been to a mall. I wondered how many of my children had told me a fib in order to protect their esteem among their peers. Since that time, I have become cautious about assuming anything regarding my students' experiences. I find it better for all concerned if I can provide the introductory activity in the classroom.

Concept Development

The concept development phase is, and has always been, a time for the teacher to provide direct instruction if needed. It is an excellent time for teachers to use multi-sensory and multi-task choices for students to learn by capitalizing on their own strength areas. Students are involved as they are guided to create explanations, classifications, or hypotheses through discussions, mini-lectures, research, models, and so forth. With the advent of the Internet, learners are literally linked to any of the best research, models, and examples they would like to explore. The key idea in the learning cycle is that although this phase has traditionally been used to introduce lessons, research tells us that it is better placed after the exploration phase. This phase is greatly enhanced by the teacher's ability to utilize effective questioning techniques.

Questions can generally be regarded as being in three levels:

1. First level *(exploration phase)*
   Students are asked to gather or recall information.

2. Second level *(concept development phase)*
   Students are asked to analyze, classify, compare, contrast, distinguish, explain, group, infer, make an analogy, organize, or synthesize.

3. Third level *(concept application phase)*
   Students are encouraged to think intuitively, creatively, and hypothetically. They may be called on to apply a principle, build a model, evaluate, extrapolate, forecast, generalize, hypothesize, imagine, judge, predict, or speculate.

Questioning is an often-overlooked strategic teaching tool. Effective questioning techniques can help the teacher discover student experiences, understandings, and misconceptions. They can also help guide student thinking and learning.

It is important to think deeply about what kinds of questions to ask students *before* teaching a lesson. Even experienced teachers and certainly novice teachers will want to write out questions they want to ask when they teach the lesson. Giving thought to the kinds of questions asked can help a teacher think about the aim of the lesson and what it is students should know and to be able to do when they leave class (e.g. the mission statement). Even hands-on, active learning experiences are not complete without a follow-up opportunity for students to clarify what they learned and extend their learning to new and novel situations. The questions posed cue students to the level of thinking expected of them.

Effective Questioning Technique Tips

- Always ask the question *before* calling on a particular student. Calling a student's name before the question is asked signals the other students that they don't have to think about it.

- Avoid bombarding students with too much "teacher talk." Strive to talk less and listen more.

- Wait time should be more than 2 seconds, and can be as long as 6 seconds. Practice to get comfortable with this technique. (Because of my Type-A personality, this was really hard for me. I used to hand a designated student—usually one who needed help to stay focused—a timer and ask her or him to help me in gauging my wait time.)

- Practice calling on ALL students. (It's harder than it seems!) Consider drawing names randomly, mark names on a seating chart as you call them, or create another way to ensure that all students are given a chance to answer at some point during the lesson. DO NOT let a few students monopolize the question-answer session.

- Give the same think time to all students! Often teachers give the perceived brighter students more time to generate an answer than those who are thought to be not so bright.

- Require students to raise their hands to be called on. This helps ensure that students are called on evenly and fairly. (It also helps students who need help in controlling impulsivity).

- It is motivating and cognitively helpful to have other students respond to or elaborate on an answer rather than always having the teacher reacting to each individual answer.

- Ask students to orally elaborate (talk out loud about their thinking process) on how they got their answers. This is a great help to students who need tips on how to make certain connections, and it promotes Higher-Order thinking.

- When giving a follow-up comment, use strong praise sparingly. It is more beneficial to have students comment on each other's answers.

- Avoid bluffing an answer to a student question for which you do not have an answer. Be a good model in problem solving to find it.

- Encourage students to ask questions about process as well as content.

(adapted from Kellough and Kellough,
Secondary School Teaching: A Guide to Methods and Resources,
Planning for Competence, 1999.)

Concept Application

According to Newmann, Marks, & Gamoran (1995), assessment strategies are moving beyond superficial levels of comprehension and towards deeper understandings such as:

- Construction of knowledge: Students should construct or produce knowledge, instead of merely reproducing or identifying understandings that others have created.

- Disciplined inquiry: Students should engage in cognitive work that requires them to rely on a field of knowledge, search for understanding, and communicate their ideas and findings in "elaborate forms."

- Value beyond school: Students' accomplishments should have value—either aesthetic, utilitarian, or personal—beyond just documenting their competence.

If educators truly want students to become autonomous, life-long learners, shouldn't they *assess* that which they say they truly value even though it is indeed harder to measure? It is certainly more difficult to create divergent tasks that compel students to apply concepts to a broader perspective. Teachers who are firmly grounded in their subject areas and who are not afraid themselves to think "outside the lines" will foster a spirit of wonder and delight in learning.

In his book, *Awakening Genius in the Classroom*, Thomas Armstrong (1998) strongly advocates models that promote a natural rhythm to learning. He is concerned about tapping the source of what drives the learning process in every child. The Learning Cycle seems to be a good fit with his twelve aspects of students' intrinsic motivation to learn—curiosity, playfulness, imagination, creativity, wonder, wisdom, inventiveness, vitality, sensitivity, flexibility, humor, and joy.

In summary, it can be said that teaching for understanding requires different strategies than traditionally used for instruction. In a lesson designed to meet the needs of many marchers, students' misconceptions are addressed through exploration and discussion. Students explore their own questions as a way of acquiring new knowledge. In the educational community, there is agreement that traditional direct teaching is not the most effective way to promote conceptual change or real understanding of new concepts. It is generally agreed that the Learning Cycle is more suited to individualizing instruction and thus more successfully meets the needs of all learners in terms of student motivation, understanding, and development of higher level thinking skills.

Lesson Plan for Dr. Silver's Class

Subject: _____

Title: _____

Grade Level: _____ Time Allotment: _____

I. Instructional Goals

General statements of desired outcomes for the learners are phrased to include a process term (verb) and a content term. (Refer to state curriculum standards.)

II. Performance Objectives

Descriptions of specific observable behaviors that students develop as a result of the learning activities. Include objectives for all domains when appropriate: cognitive, affective, psychomotor, and social. For the cognitive domain, include higher-level objectives as well as those at the knowledge level.

III. Teaching/Learning Procedures

Time _____

Activity _____

___ A. Motivation/Introduction

Present how you will capture the students' attention, relate the topic to their lives, and/or relate to past lessons.

___ B. Teaching/Learning Activities

Describe the sequence of activities that you will use to teach the lesson.

Drumming to the Beat of a Different Marcher
© *2003 by Incentive Publications, Inc., Nashville, TN*

Exploration Phase

Identify the open-ended questions or explorations that provide a common experience to initiate students' interaction with information, materials, and/or each other.

Concept Development Phase

Describe how you will expand vocabulary, utilize direct instruction, and incorporate the investigation of other resources; connect skills practice to the goal.

Concept Application Phase

Explain how students will be required to apply new knowledge to "real world" and/or new situations.

___ C. Closure

Clarify how you will provide a summary of the key concepts in the lesson. Show how you will bring together past, present, and future learning.

IV. Material/Media

Include a variety of materials other than the textbook. Use materials that appeal to Multiple Intelligences.

V. Supplemental Activities

Describe any accommodations you will make for diverse learners.

Lesson-related activities can include computer programs, learning centers, activity folders, educational games, peer tutoring, and other methods for helping special students master the concept/skills.

(Adapted from *Louisiana Tech University's Student Teacher Handbook*)

Lesson Plan Template

Subject: _____

Title: _____

Grade Level: _____ Time Allotment: _____

I.   Instructional Goals

_____

_____

_____

II. Performance Objectives

_____

_____

_____

III. Teaching/Learning Procedures

Time _____

Activity _____

___ A. Motivation/Introduction

___ B. Teaching/Learning Activities

Exploration Phase:

Concept Development Phase:

Concept Application Phase:

___ C. Closure

IV. Material/Media

V. Supplemental Activities

(Adapted from *Louisiana Tech University's*
Student Teacher Handbook)

In order to make sure a lesson plan follows the learning cycle model, use the following checklist:

Learning Cycle Checklist

Exploration Phase

- [ ] 1. The lesson begins with an engaging activity, provocative question, or interesting observation that provides or draws on a common experience.

- [ ] 2. The students are given sufficient time to interact with the materials and/or explore open-ended questions.

- [ ] 3. Students are asked to collect and organize data.

Conceptual Development Phase

- [ ] 1. Explanations are based on emerging patterns observed in the exploration phase.

- [ ] 2. The concepts and vocabulary developed are natural outgrowths of the exploration activity.

- [ ] 3. Questions have been designed to purposefully move students towards deeper understandings and meanings.

Concept Application Phase

- [ ] 1. Students interact with one another and compare ideas and explanations.

- [ ] 2. Students are required to apply newly learned concepts to "real life" situations.

- [ ] 3. Assessments are designed that allow students to demonstrate their ability to use newly acquired information and skills in novel and unique ways.

Drumming to the Beat of a Different Marcher
©2003 by Incentive Publications, Inc., Nashville, TN

> *It's not so much that we're afraid of change or so in love with the old ways, but it's that place in-between that we fear. It's like being between trapezes. It's Linus when his blanket is in the dryer. There's nothing to hold on to."*
> – Marilyn Ferguson, *The Aquarian Conspiracy*

Redesigning an instructional and assessment strategy to incorporate the Learning Cycle is well worth the effort. However, it does take time and considerable thought. The curriculum resources and textbooks currently used may already be based on this model; if so, the job will be much easier. Some subjects are easier to adapt to this model than others. Whatever the case, take the time to give serious thought to how to ensure that all students will have a reasonable chance to progress towards the intended outcomes. Do not try to redesign all class lessons at one time. First, redo lessons that easily lend themselves to this model. Then, over time try to change the majority of what is taught to incorporate at least some aspects of the learning cycle. Constantly reflect on what is working and what is not. Keep the things that are, and change the things that are not.

Tips for Instituting Reform Practices in Your Classroom

- Don't try to do it all at once. Start with one idea, then try another.

- Don't try to do it alone. Involve other teachers, parents, and administrators.

- Get involved in your professional networking especially through your subject area organizations. Read their journals, attend their workshops, subscribe to their newsletters, and visit their recommended sites on the Internet.

- Use the Internet to find new ideas, talk with other teachers, and ask questions you may have.

- Talk with others about the changes being made. Let parents, students, and other teachers know what is happening.

- Communicate with business and industry for practical ideas about real-life assessment practices.

- Enjoy the process. Reflect on successes as well as failures.

Adapted from the 1991 National Council for Teachers of Math (NCTM) booklet *Mathematics Assessment: Myths, Models, Good Questions, and Practical Suggestions*

On Learning

> *Learning is finding out what you already know.*
> *Doing is demonstrating that you know it.*
> *Teaching is reminding others that they know it just as well as you.*
> *You are all learners, doers, teachers.*
> – Richard Bach

Recommended Reading List

Jackson, Anthony W., and Gayle A. Davis. *Turning Points 2000: Educating Adolescents in the 21st Century.* NY: Teachers College Press, 2000.

Tomlinson, Carol A. *The Differentiated Classroom: Responding to the Needs of All Learners.* Alexandria, VA: Association for Supervision and Curriculum Development (ASCD), 1999.

Wiggins, Grant, and Jay McTighe. *Understanding by Design.* Alexandria, VA: Association for Supervision and Curriculum Development (ASCD), 1998.

Chapter 4

Multiple Intelligences and Different Learning Styles
If They All Have Gifts, Why Don't They Open Them?

I am often asked if I support the gifted education program. My response has always been that I think the gifted curriculum is exceptional and definitely should be available—to everyone. It is my belief that all children really do have gifts. I think that it is the responsibility of educators to "go in after" vastly different students—armed with best practices and with educational plans customized to meet their specific needs.

One way that we can tap more of the gifts in students is to provide them with divergent opportunities for success. Two powerful theories that strengthen the call for varied teaching strategies and assessment are those of Multiple Intelligences (MIs) and learning styles. My favorite educational maxim for the decade comes from Howard Gardner, MI researcher, who popularized the notion that:

> *It's not about how smart they are, it's about how they are smart.*
> – Howard Gardner

All students have abilities, but in our naive belief that some strengths and learning styles are more valuable than others, we have excluded many learners from feeling capable and from being successful. Students who don't learn it "the right way" are told that they will have to do it again and try harder next time. Remediation in this traditional sense is a bit ridiculous. If a student cannot correctly do the first 25 problem sets given to her/him, why assign 25 more of the exact same thing? Why not try something entirely different? I much prefer the idea of compensation, which is helping students learn to use their strengths to work around the areas in which they are struggling. Most teachers truly want to include all students, but they are often unsure how to do it.

(Inclusive vs. Exclusive Teacher)

I help them learn how they are smart.
I test how slow they are.
I like it if their ways depart.
I just want what is par.

I try to differentiate.
I give them all one task.
My role is to accommodate.
They ought to do what's asked.

Effective teaching is my creed
We get through every text.
I give them all the time they need
Slow learners have me vexed.

I must address each learning style.
I show them one right way.
Exciting methods get a trial.
I don't have time to play!

Alternative assessment's great.
I only need one test.
With students I collaborate.
Goal setting I detest!

Assignments are not uniform.
We're all on the same page.
My teaching methods show reform.
I don't "improve with age!"

I want to get them in "the flow."
I wish they understood . . .
So they'll have fun with what they know.
I'd teach them if I could.

Andy's Story

Sometimes I am such a hypocrite. I constantly tell adults to listen carefully to the voice within each child, yet I failed to do exactly that when my youngest stepson, Andy, told me that he wanted to be a musician. He had never had a music lesson, been in band, or even played an instrument (unless you count spoons, pencils, and any other utensils that could be commandeered for an impromptu percussion performance). Being a seasoned middle school teacher, I am very familiar with the drummings and tappings of adolescent boys. I ignored Andy and hoped that he would "grow out of it." One day, he asked me if I would help talk his dad into buying him a set of snare drums.

I vividly remember my warm and caring reply, "Now let me see if I have this straight, Andy. We have 5 boys, 4 of whom are teenagers, and your thinking is that what we are missing in this house is a set of SNARE DRUMS! I don't think so!"

Undaunted, young Mr. Silver got a job and earned enough money to buy the drums himself. Very soon after he began playing real drums it became obvious that not only did he have a musical intelligence, he is musically gifted. He had told all of the adults in his life this fact for years, but none of us had paid any attention to him.

Now here's the amazing part. Before Andy came to live with his dad and me in the eighth grade, he had been tested and labeled as a slow, low-level learner. Previous educators told his parents that the prognosis for his success was not good because he was such a poor reader. One teacher had even commented that Andy would probably never graduate from high school.

When we enrolled him in the local school where my own sons attended, we were informed that his records indicated a need for special classes. The label a group of educators had so easily placed on him when he was in the second grade deeply disturbed me. In spending time with my stepson, I had come to realize that Andy was extremely perceptive as well as an uncommonly deep thinker. We wanted him put in regular education classes with his peers at his new school. The administrators balked, but because I know the law and how the system works, I was able to get Andy placed where we wanted him. Despite his very low standardized test scores and his documented learning disabilities (dyslexia, among others) he was placed in regular classes with his peers. I felt temporarily vindicated until a thought hit me: What happens to the children who have no advocate? What becomes of students who start believing the labels put on them?

Even being placed in regular classes in a new school with a new start was not a simple solution for Andy. Years of being both overtly and covertly told that he was not as promising as the others had taken its toll on him. He had lost his spirit for trying because it was so hard for him to learn in a R3 (read, recite, regurgitate) world. In the few classes he had that teachers actually let him do something (rather than just read from the text and answer questions) he did fairly well. In classes where teachers encouraged passionate debates about interesting issues, Andy soared. But classes such as those were the exception, and most of the time he was required to listen, take notes, memorize, and write about what he remembered being told. He really tried, but he told me he just could not get the information to "stick."

It was the music that turned things around for our young percussionist/learner. When he began playing in earnest, he would study while tapping out rhythms. The long passages of narrative that Andy struggled to remember came easily to him when he attached the desired information to the drum riffs he would later play back in his head during class. He used his musical ability to remember facts and important data. It worked! (How many of us still sing the "A B C Song" in our heads when filing papers?) The more success he had in school, the harder he tried. He eventually taught himself to use his music as a compensatory study skill to help him remember all kinds of things. This kid who was "never going to graduate from high school" ended up graduating on time, with his class, and with honors! At the graduation ceremony, his mom leaned over and thanked me. I quickly pointed out that I appreciated her sentiment, but it was Andy who was the one responsible for his success. He found his own voice, his own step, his own rhythm.

After this "kid who was never going to graduate from high school" was awarded the John Phillips Sousa Music Award his senior year, he went to college on a music scholarship, studied to be an astro-geologist (okay, a rock star), finished college on the dean's list with a degree in jazz performance and a certification to teach. Andy is now a successful musician in Austin, Texas who teaches part-time and loves his life.

Andy actually helped crystallize for me what I had known intuitively for quite a while. Sometimes students who have difficulty memorizing large chunks of narrative can easily recall information that is put to a beat or a melody. Many teachers were creating raps, patters, and songs to help reinforce tedious information long before Multiple Intelligence proponents came along to tell us why it worked. One teacher I know had her high school biology students make up a musical square dance that demonstrated how cells divide. They sang and danced their way through the process of mitosis with relative ease, and I doubt one of them will ever forget the names of the organelles or the sequence of the phases. (To learn more about the power of attaching new learning to music, read Don Campbell's *The Mozart Effect*.)

But musical intelligence is just one of the ways that students can be smart. There are at least seven others. Effective teachers have been using a kind of Multiple Intelligence lesson design for years when they let students act out the molecules or create a mural of a historical timeline or present a first person oral book report. Good teachers have always found ways to honor student abilities and incorporate them into effective instruction and assessment.

The good news is that educators today don't have to start from scratch. A myriad of information is available about how to integrate Multiple Intelligences into lessons through our professional journals, the Internet, and in-service training. Scores of books and Web sites with lesson plans for teaching and assessing with Multiple Intelligences are now available. Beware of blindly adopting a prepackaged lesson design and missing the depth of what Gardner has offered us. The point of Multiple Intelligences is to assist teachers in creating the best learning experiences possible for each student. It is a very individual process that cannot be duplicated mechanically.

Multiple Intelligences theory is being discussed and used in ever-widening educational circles. A cornerstone to the principle that "no child will be left behind" is the premise that students' intelligences will be identified (they all have strengths in at least one or two areas) and used to maximize their understandings of the world around them. Helping them learn to capitalize on their competencies is a key way of inspiring them to be lifelong learners. Researchers are finding more and more that when students are taught and assessed using their strongest areas for even a small part of the school day, their overall learning and performance is enhanced.

Howard Gardner's Multiple Intelligences

Howard Gardner first described seven intelligences in his 1983 book, *Frames of Mind*. He said then that his research findings represented his "best-faith effort" to identify intelligence less as a single entity and more as a multi-dimensional model that can be identified through empirical findings dealing with neurobiology, cultural history, and cognitive psychology. He acknowledged then that no empirically based theory is ever established permanently and said that his theory would be revised if new findings from the laboratory and from the field emerged. True to his word, Gardner added an eighth intelligence to his list in 1995.

Gardner did not write his Multiple Intelligences theory with an educational end in mind. He has often commented that he is as surprised as anyone at how quickly the education community embraced his findings. He has urged users of his theory to adhere to three tenets (1995):

1) cultivate skills that are valued in the community and society
2) approach new concepts and subjects in a variety of ways
3) personalize instruction as much as possible

Gardner believes that the best use of his research findings is for teachers to recognize students' individual ways of being smart. He urges teachers to help students use their distinct combinations of intelligences to be successful in school and in life.

Summary of the Eight Intelligences

Checkley (1997) offers Gardner's summary of the eight intelligences:

- **Linguistic intelligence** is the capacity to use language, your native language, and perhaps other languages, to express what is on your mind and to understand other people. Poets really specialize in linguistic intelligence, but any kind of writer, orator, speaker, lawyer, or a person for whom language is an important stock in trade highlights linguistic intelligence.

- People with a highly developed **logical-mathematical intelligence** understand the underlying principles of some kind of a causal system, the way a scientist or a logician does; or can manipulate numbers, quantities, and operations, the way a mathematician does.

- **Spatial intelligence** refers to the ability to represent the spatial world internally in your mind—the way a sailor or airplane pilot navigates the large spatial world, or the way a chess player or sculptor represents a more circumscribed spatial world. Spatial intelligence can be used in the arts or in the sciences. If you are spatially intelligent and oriented toward the arts, you are more likely to become a painter or sculptor or an architect than, say, a musician or a writer. Similarly, certain sciences like anatomy or topology emphasize spatial intelligence.

- **Bodily kinesthetic intelligence** is the capacity to use your whole body or parts of you body—your hand, your fingers, your arms—to solve a problem, make something, or put on some kind of a production. The most evident examples are people in athletics or the performing arts, particularly dance or acting.

- **Musical intelligence** is the capacity to think in music, to be able to hear patterns, recognize them, remember them, and perhaps manipulate them. People who have a strong musical intelligence don't just remember music easily—they can't get it out of their minds because it's so omnipresent. Now, some people will say, "Yes, music is important, but it's a talent." And I say, "Fine, let's call it a talent." But, then we have to leave the word "intelligent" out of all discussions of human abilities.

- **Interpersonal intelligence** is understanding other people. It's an ability we all need, but is at a premium if you are a teacher, clinician, salesperson, or politician. Anybody who deals with other people has to be skilled in the interpersonal sphere.

- **Intra-personal intelligenc**e refers to having an understanding of yourself, of knowing who you are, what you can do, what you want to do, how you react to things, which things to avoid, and which things to gravitate toward. We are drawn to people who have a good understanding of themselves because those people tend not to screw up. They tend to know what they can do. They tend to know what they can't do. And they tend to know where to go if they need help.

- **Naturalist intelligence** designates the human ability to discriminate among living things (plants, animals) as well as sensitivity to other features of the natural world (clouds, rock configurations). This ability was clearly of value in our evolutionary past as hunters, gatherers, and farmers; it continues to be central in such roles as botanist or chef. I also speculate that much of our consumer society exploits the naturalist intelligences, which can be mobilized in the discrimination among cars, sneakers, kinds of makeup, and the like.

Students like to construct their own intelligence profiles using various inventories. An in-depth consideration of his or her major strength areas is a valuable metacognitive tool for students. There are several Multiple Intelligences inventories available in current literature as well as on the Internet.

I wrote the following icebreaker activity to introduce students to the concept of Multiple Intelligences. When using it, remind students that one can be strong in "part of" an intelligence and not so strong in the other components. Each of these indicators represents only one area of an intelligence; there are many more.

Name: _____

Essential Eight

The purpose of this "get acquainted" activity is to start thinking about the different areas of intelligence. Participants are to mix freely and try to get seven different people to sign the blanks (each participant may sign his or her own sheet once). In order to record a name in the blank, the person signing must actually perform the task (not just say that she or he can do it).

Find Someone Who Can:

_____ finish this numerical sequence:
64, 1, 49, 4, 36, 9, 25, _____
and explain the logic behind it.   *(number smart)*

_____ honestly say that he or she has more
strengths than weaknesses, and name
6 strengths in less than 15 seconds.   *(self smart)*

_____ hum the first line of *Silent Night* on key.   *(music smart)*

_____ recite a poem from memory.   *(word smart)*

_____ with hands on head stand on one foot
with eyes closed for at least 7 seconds.   *(body smart)*

_____ name five very close friends
in less than 8 seconds.   *(people smart)*

_____ recall at least one dream
from the last 3 weeks.   *(picture smart)*

_____ within 20 seconds name 6 ways
to sort rocks into categories.   *(nature smart)*

(c) Debbie Silver, 1998

After we do the icebreaker, I ask students if some of the tasks are more appealing to them than others. They always answer in the affirmative. I explain to them that research has now alerted us to the fact that everyone is smart in at least one or two of the eight intelligences, and no one is inordinately smart in all eight.

To illustrate this I explain to them about idiot savants who show dramatic abilities in one area and very little ability in others. Most of them have seen the movie *Rain Man*, so they have a visual image of how this can occur. I tell them that to a less extraordinary degree, all humans are more highly advanced in one or two intelligences than in the others.

While everyone has some quantity of every intelligence, certain areas will be intrinsically easier for them. All students have a unique blend of ranges and combinations of the eight intelligences. Given that an individual can improve every intelligence area with effort, everyone should work to improve the areas where she or he is not so strong while capitalizing on the areas that are.

To help them ascertain their individual strength areas, I give them a profile to fill out. Profiles are beneficial in helping students discover the areas where they are smart (if the term "intelligence" is troubling, think of it as areas of strength, areas in which the student demonstrates a pre-dispositional leaning, or groups of tasks which see to come easily for the student). Inventory checklists can be used to determine strengths and help individuals understand their own potential.

Teacher checklists are useful for making observations about students. It is useful for educators to get a sense about the strengths of each child in order to help design appropriate instructional and assessment strategies. No one is advocating that every concept be taught in eight different ways, but the point is to realize that any important topic can be and probably should be taught in more than one way.

Checklists for Assessing "How Students Are Smart"

Name of Student: _____

Check all the items that apply:

Linguistic Intelligence
(Word Smart)

☐ 1. Is a good reader
☐ 2. Enjoys word games
☐ 3. Is a good joke teller/storyteller
☐ 4. Has a good vocabulary
☐ 5. Enjoys listening to stories and/or poems
☐ 6. Likes to write stories and/or poems
☐ 7. Communicates with others in a highly verbal way
☐ 8. Appreciates rhymes, puns, and/or nonsense words
☐ 9. Has a good memory for words, stories, details

Other linguistic strengths:

_____
_____
_____

Logical-Mathematical Intelligence
(Number Smart)

☐ 1. Asks a lot of questions about how things work
☐ 2. Has a good sense of cause and effect
☐ 3. Finds math games interesting
☐ 4. Can see and repeat patterns easily
☐ 5. Enjoys working puzzles and brain teasers
☐ 6. Understands computer programming
☐ 7. Is a logical thinker
☐ 8. Can estimate things involving numbers with relative ease
☐ 9. Can work math concepts in head

Other logical-mathematical strengths:

_____
_____
_____

Visual-Spatial Intelligence
(Picture Smart)

☐ 1. Reports clear, visual images (or dreams)
☐ 2. Can envision objects from more than one perspective
☐ 3. Daydreams more than peers
☐ 4. Likes to draw and/or create art projects
☐ 5. Has a good eye for detail and color
☐ 6. Is good at spatial games like chess and Tetris
☐ 7. Likes movies, slides, or other visual presentations
☐ 8. Can move between 2-dimensional and 3-dimensional representations with ease
☐ 9. Can read and/or create maps

Other visual-spatial strengths:

_____
_____
_____

Bodily-Kinesthetic Intelligence
(Body Smart)

☐ 1. Is very coordinated
☐ 2. Exceptionally mobile: moves, twitches, fidgets, taps when seated for long
☐ 3. Enjoys working with clay, finger-paint, and other tactile media
☐ 4. Can mimic others' gestures, posture, and movements
☐ 5. Must touch anything new or interesting
☐ 6. Loves to take things apart and put them back together
☐ 7. Uses dramatic body movements for self-expression
☐ 8. Enjoys running, hopping, climbing, wrestling, or similar activities
☐ 9. Exhibits fine motor control (crafts, painting, etc.)

Other bodily-kinesthetic strengths:

_____
_____
_____

Musical Intelligence
(Music Smart)

- [ ] 1. Can detect music that is off-key, off-beat, or disturbing in some way
- [ ] 2. Remembers melodies of songs
- [ ] 3. Taps rhythmically as he/she works or plays
- [ ] 4. Sensitive to environmental noise (rain on the windows, etc.)
- [ ] 5. Plays a musical instrument and/or sings in a choir.
- [ ] 6. Has a good singing voice
- [ ] 7. Responds favorably when music is played
- [ ] 8. Sings songs that he/she has learned
- [ ] 9. Unconsciously hums much of the time

Other musical strengths:

_____
_____
_____

Interpersonal Communications Intelligence *(People Smart)*

- [ ] 1. Establishes meaningful peer relationships
- [ ] 2. Seems to be a natural leader
- [ ] 3. Empathizes with others
- [ ] 4. Likes to play with others
- [ ] 5. Shows good teamwork skills
- [ ] 6. Others seek this student's company
- [ ] 7. Has two or more close friends
- [ ] 8. Frequently acts as a mediator and/or peace maker
- [ ] 9. Enjoys teaching others

Other interpersonal communication strengths:

_____
_____
_____

Intra-personal Awareness Intelligence
(Self Smart)

- [ ] 1. Displays a sense of strong will
- [ ] 2. Enjoys playing or working alone
- [ ] 3. Has high self-esteem
- [ ] 4. Has a good sense of self-direction
- [ ] 5. Does not mind being different from others
- [ ] 6. Has a realistic view of his or her strengths and weaknesses
- [ ] 7. Is able to deal effectively with successes and failures
- [ ] 8. Has an interest or talent that is not readily shared with others
- [ ] 9. Seems to "march to the beat of a different drummer"

Other intra-personal awareness strengths:

_____
_____
_____

Naturalistic Intelligence
(Nature Smart)

- [ ] 1. Likes to identify and classify living and nonliving things in nature
- [ ] 2. Cares for pets or animals
- [ ] 3. Understands repeating patterns in nature and the universe
- [ ] 4. Seems more "in tune with nature" than peers
- [ ] 5. Would rather be outside than inside
- [ ] 6. Has a demonstrated appreciation for a part of the natural world (i.e., dinosaurs, clouds, rocks, etc.)
- [ ] 7. Likes to garden and/or appreciates plants
- [ ] 8. Understands and appreciates the environment
- [ ] 9. Loves to collect things from nature

Other naturalistic strengths:

_____
_____
_____

Adapted by Debbie Silver from *Multiple Intelligences in the Classroom* by Thomas Armstrong (1994)

Drumming to the Beat of a Different Marcher
© *2003 by Incentive Publications, Inc., Nashville, TN*

Gardner maintains that learning is a consequence of thinking—and good thinking is learnable by all students. He believes that learning should include deep understanding, which involves the flexible, active use of knowledge. Gardner contends that students should both receive instruction using Multiple Intelligence strategies, and, just as importantly, be assessed using the same strategies.

Undertaking alternative assessment takes creativity, thoughtful planning, and time. As with all new approaches, teachers should start with incremental steps and proceed at a comfortable pace. Doing something innovative occasionally takes a little public relations groundwork with students, colleagues, administrators, and parents. Ask them to withhold judgment until plans are fully implemented. Be ready to coach them through the process and listen attentively to their apprehensions. It is important that teachers ask for their patience. Eventually, most of their concerns will be assuaged. It is hard to argue with success, and customizing teaching to fit selected outcomes will eventually lead to enhanced learning for all students.

There are literally hundreds of books and resources available to educators who wish to find ideas for developing inventive ways that allow students to demonstrate their genuine understandings. My best advice is to use prepackaged programs only as guides. Generally, teachers should adapt the work of others to fit their exact needs. Give deep thought to what essential ideas and skills students will be taught to master.

Many teachers brainstorm with students about how best to find out what they understand. They let them help develop the standards and expectations for demonstrating their knowledge of a desired concept as well as the rubric that will determine their progress towards the goal. Finally, educators should seek to give students options about how they will show what they know and can do. Not every assessment has to be designed to give students eight different ways of demonstrating success, but at least occasionally students need to have choices other than traditional paper and pencil. Here are just a few ideas for starters:

Different Ways to Find Out What Students Understand

Make a chart or diagram	Do a demonstration	Create a dance
Write a letter to the editor	Make a scrapbook	Design a Web Quest
Conduct a discussion	Participate in a debate	Create a puppet show
Create an advertisement	Make an editorial video	Keep a journal log
Write an essay	Design a structure	Create a report
Participate in a simulation	Develop a collection	Make a plan
Create a poem	Write and do a rap	Make a mural
Do a photo essay	Design a game	Create a new product
Create an invention	Present a news report	Do an experiment
Teach someone else	Judge an event	Make a model
Write an analogy	Conduct an interview	Develop a rubric
Participate in a mock trial	Create cartoons	Write a book
Design and teach a class	Create a flow chart	Make a learning center
Devise a new recipe	Give a performance	Draw a blueprint
Write a monologue	Defend a theory	Do a self-assessment
Illustrate a math concept	Create a brochure	Solve a mystery
Do a multimedia presentation	Develop an exhibit	Critique a book

Do a Gallery Walk (Carousel Walk)

Write a diary from the perspective of someone else

Set up a system of checks and balances

Multiple Intelligence Theory has done much to advance the argument for differentiated instruction. No thinking person can acknowledge that children have unique blends of the eight intelligences and then advocate that they all be taught the same thing at the same time in the same way. Along that same line we should concentrate on finding valid ways of assessing what students know that are not entirely based on literacy skills.

Howard Gardner has stated repeatedly that he does not think his identified levels of intelligence should be used to label or sort remedial students. The knowledge that students are smart in different ways should empower teachers to seek conduits for each child's optimum opportunities for learning. The self-knowledge that "they are smart, too" encourages students to feel competent and to become successful learners.

Learning Styles

Another strong argument for differentiated instruction comes from the field of psychology. Behavioral and cognitive psychologists have long maintained that students come to school with certain inherent learning styles, many of which are at absolutely odds with traditional teaching methods.

Before we knew about Multiple Intelligence, teachers were encouraged by researchers to be mindful that students have fixed ways of internalizing new information. Educators were told that not all students learned equally well with traditional teaching strategies. (I wasn't worried; there was nothing traditional about the way I taught!)

I am embarrassed to admit it, but I was in my thirties before I discovered a very important lesson about my "outside-the-lines" teaching style. For years I had the condescending belief that if everyone would just "chill out" and approach life with the same spontaneous light hearted attitude I had, the world would be a better place. I patiently tried to deal with my very best friend (a teacher, of course) who made lists of her lists and organized her life with all the passion of a tax auditor. She often became frustrated with my attempts to skip her planned meetings (I would rather try to tie rattlesnakes in knots than go to a meeting) and was frequently impatient with my lack of preparation and disregard for details. Likewise I was regularly put off by her need to address every possible contingency with a "back-up plan," and laughed about her calendar that looked like a strategic military plan. Basically I balked at her attempts to control me, and she cringed at what she saw as my flightiness and irresponsibility.

In my classroom, I had similar difficulties with students who wanted to know exactly what, when, and how I was going to teach, like the student who came to my sixth grade class on the first day of school and wanted a syllabus of what we'd be doing for the rest of the year! (I refrained from telling her my first thought—that people in Hell want ice water, but that doesn't mean they're going to get it.) I was annoyed that she put me on the spot like that for something so entirely unnecessary. I knew this was going to be a long year.

It really used to bother me that after I spent extraordinary time and energy making a lesson fun and exciting some child would ask, "Aren't we supposed to be doing our spelling words now?" I wanted to choke him! It disturbed me when I told students like that to just relax because I would make sure we got around to everything, but they would still be uptight. It troubled me when students would ask, "Is this going to be on the test?" My answer that they should enjoy the learning and not worry about the test did not seem to soothe them at all. There was a definite rub between a few of my students and me that I attributed to their inability to trust me and just loosen up.

Then, as a part of a professional improvement program, my very best friend and I drove to the Big City to attend a conference on learning styles. I had never even heard of learning styles, but I'm always in need of styling tips, so I jumped at the chance to go. The two of us were introduced to the presenter, Dr. Anthony Gregorc, who had all the participants take his Style Delineator™ (1982). The instrument had a bunch of words that we were to rate from 4–1 according to our personal thoughts and feelings. We used our scores to graph our tendencies for the way we handled the immediate demands on our lives. I peeked to look at my friend's graph and was not at all surprised to see that hers was the exact opposite of mine.

When Dr. Gregorc asked for a show of hands from the participants whose highest score was in the abstract random (his term) group, I proudly shot my arm up. My friend looked quite dejected as our instructor told everyone to look around at those who had their hands up because we were the ones who tended to be the most fun, spontaneous people in the room. I beamed as he explained that others generally liked to be around us because we are so colorful. I was ready for him to let the rest of the group know that they should all strive to be like us AR's when he added, "By the way, these folks have no concept of time, they are terrible with details, and they frustrate the heck out of those of you who are trying to plan important things." I shrank in my chair as my friend looked over smugly and said under her breath, "You got that right, Doc!"

Dr. Gregorc went on to point out the strengths and the weaknesses of his four categories: abstract random, abstract sequential, concrete random, and concrete sequential. All four categories, not just mine, were balanced by strong positive features as well as inherent limitations. He told us that the way people internalize information and approach problem solving is static and instinctive.

It was like an epiphany for me. I suddenly realized that when others would not cooperate and do it my way, it wasn't so much that they were trying to subvert me personally, but rather that they were trying to use practices with which they were the most comfortable. When learners complained that they couldn't do it the way I showed them, it was more a matter of style than a matter of intelligence or compliance.

I listened intently to what my new prophet said. I took notes, asked questions, and later did follow-up research on the topic of learning styles. It totally changed the way I was teaching. I realized that I had been utilizing only the instructional methods that I found appealing. Because I am very random and do not like extensive reading assignments, drill and practice, going step-by-step, or any kind of rigid strategies, I simply did not use them. Because I am so abstract in my thinking, I never saw the need to use a chalkboard, an overhead projector, outlines, or even class notes. My frenzied and unpredictable teaching techniques were fine for my abstract random students, but I suddenly understood that those who were more sequential and concrete were getting left out. No wonder they had seemed so bothered and confused by my frantic pace. It was time to change some of my practices.

Since that significant day, I have done considerable research on the topic of learning styles. I found that the concept of four basic personality types has its roots in ancient history and philosophy. Swiss psychologist Carl Jung (1923) popularized the division of personalities into four categories; thinking, sensing, feeling, and intuitive. Since that time, numerous psychometric instruments have been developed that basically attribute central human tendencies to four major groups. The MBTI® (Myers-Briggs Type Indicator) distinguishes areas similar to Jung's; extroverted/introverted, intuitive/sensing, feeling/thinking, perceiving/judging.

Silver, Strong & Associates, Inc. (1980) identify areas similar to Jung's: sensing/thinking (mastery style), sensing/feeling (interpersonal style), intuitive/thinking (understanding style), intuitive/feeling (self-expressive style). Religious writer Florence Littauer (1986) has spoken at length on her four categories: sanguine, choleric, melancholy, and phlegmatic. A current popular testing/training program is that of True Colors®, which uses colors to indicate these personality distinctions; courageous, conventional, compassionate, conceptual. And there are many others.

The important thing I learned from my research and my subsequent revision of my own teaching practices is that, whatever the classification, there is demonstrable evidence that different learners can best be taught through identified instructional strategies and assessments. Teachers can most effectively engage each and every learner by adapting differentiated approaches.

Most of the learning style inventories and categories I have studied have the same theoretical underpinnings as the one by Dr. Gregorc. I will use his categories to illustrate my points because his are the ones with which I am most familiar.

The following classifications are the property of Dr. Anthony Gregorc. They have emerged from his extensive research on the topic of learning styles. A full presentation of this material is available online.

Gregorc's 4 Basic Learning Styles

- The Abstract Random
- The Concrete Sequential
- The Abstract Sequential
- The Concrete Random

The Abstract Random

The Abstract Random learner's approach to change is subject to emotions and level of interest. His or her approach to life is idealistic, emotional, and always intense. This learner prefers an environment that allows emotional and physical freedom, is active, and is vibrant. She or he is distinguishable by attention to human behavior and an extraordinary ability to sense and interpret feelings. He or she prefers to receive information in an unstructured manner, and is therefore, comfortable in groups and with busy environments. She or he tends to evaluate all experiences "as a whole" and see the world in "black and white."

Appropriate Instructional Strategies
for the Abstract Random Learner

- Role playing
- Team games
- Short reading assignments
- Discussions
- Videos
- Peer tutoring
- Group investigations
- Active, busy environments

The Concrete Sequential

The Concrete Sequential learner is usually slow and hesitant about change. This learner's approach to life is realistic, patient, and conservative. He or she prefers an environment that is ordered, quiet, and stable. She or he has a finely tuned ability to derive information through direct, hands-on experience. This person has an extraordinary development of the five senses and likes touchable concrete materials. This student likes step-by-step directions when confronted with a new situation. He or she does not like surprises and prefers to be in control of most situations. She or he is the one learner who not only looks for directions but follows them!

Appropriate Instructional Strategies
for the Concrete Sequential Learner

- Step-by-step directions
- Workbooks
- Drill and practice
- Lectures with demonstrations
- Labeling drawings and models
- Well-structured field trips
- Color-coded study organizers
- Logical sequencing
- Focused, quiet environments

The Abstract Sequential

The Abstract Sequential learner is indecisive about change. This person focuses on knowledge and facts; he or she insists upon documentation before "buying into" new ideas. His or her approach to life is realistic, serious, logically intellectual, and determined. He or she likes an environment that is mentally stimulating but non-authoritative. She or he likes to direct his or her own learning. This student has excellent decoding abilities in the areas of written, verbal, and image symbols. He or she has a preference for presentations that are rational and have substance. She or he pays attention to detail and usually prefers to work alone.

Appropriate Instructional Strategies
for the Abstract Sequential Learner

- Extensive reading assignments
- Lecture with time for reflection
- Debate
- Essays
- Logic Problems
- Research-based lessons
- Finding information on the World Wide Web
- Individual projects
- Journaling
- Inquiry-based activities
- Quiet, well-controlled environments

The Concrete Random

The Concrete Random learner is open and amenable to change; this person is sometimes the instigator of change. His or her approach to life is inquisitive and independent. He or she likes an environment that is competitive and stimulus-rich. This person has an experimental attitude that is often accompanied by a trial-and-error approach to problem solving. She or he gets the gist of ideas quickly and demonstrates the uncanny ability to make intuitive leaps in exploring unstructured problem-solving experiences. This person is often self-motivated and not interested in details.

Appropriate Instructional Strategies
for the Concrete Random Learner

- Independent study projects
- Learning games
- Simulations
- Optional reading assignments
- Open-ended discussions
- Divergent thinking activities
- Unstructured exploration time
- Mini-lectures
- Activities on the Internet
- Moderately active environments

Please do not think that I am suggesting that teachers must cover every concept in four different styles (or eight different intelligences or a combination of both). That would be impossible as well as counterproductive. Part of the job as an educator is to prepare students for the real world, and quite frankly, in most cases, our learners will have to conform to the edicts of the real world rather than the other way around.

Rather, I suggest that by designing a variety of experiences for students as each unit is planned, teachers are more likely to appeal to their "distant drummers" and re-engage them in the learning process. It is a matter of purposefully planning lessons that offer a range of ways to internalize new information. For most of us, it is easy to plan activities in keeping with our own styles. The challenge is to blend activities that capitalize on each of the styles. (If you work on a team on which different styles are represented, this job becomes much easier.) The key is variety in ways that information is presented. Plan for how students will practice processing it and create opportunities for them to demonstrate what they know. Teachers must be diligent in giving each student a chance at using his or her own best resources.

Some people are confused by the association between learning styles and Multiple Intelligences. I use Multiple Intelligence theory in regard to content matters and learning style theory to explain matters of process. It is my belief that learning styles are a fixed mode of understanding that the learner primarily uses to master new skills and concepts. I think that a person's learning style transcends all intelligence levels. There are those who argue about the relationship between Multiple Intelligence and Learning Styles theories. Some psychologists, like Silver, Strong & Perini (2000), have tried to link Multiple Intelligences with learning styles in individuals. So far, I am not satisfied with attempts to connect them, and I don't think they have to be linked. What I do know is that students learn in unique ways, and it is to everyone's benefit if teachers are encouraged to vary techniques, strategies, assignments, and assessments so that all students have a reasonable chance at success.

> *If a doctor, lawyer, or dentist had 40 people in his office at one time, all of whom had different needs, and some of whom didn't want to be there and were causing trouble, and the doctor, lawyer, dentist, without assistance, had to treat them all with professional excellence for nine months, then he might have some conception of the classroom teacher's job.*
> – Donald D. Quinn

Flow

Sometimes when students are engaged in activities and assessments that are well matched to their individual needs a wonderful thing happens. They don't hear the bell ring, they don't want to leave class, and they carry their love for learning away from the classroom with them. This ideal state is called "flow" and is considered by many theorists and educators as the best possible learning state.

Last summer my stepson, Andy (the kid who was once told by a teacher that he was "not a strong enough reader to graduate from high school") called to ask me a question about Mihalyi Csikszentmihalyi's (pronounced "me-high chick-SENT-me-high") concept of "flow." Andy was struggling through one of Csikszentmihalyi's books because he was interested in promoting a flow state in his music students. I was very impressed. Most of the time, I cannot even get my graduate students to tackle the manuscripts of this researcher, but on his own Andy Silver was plodding through Csikszentmihalyi's theory so that he could improve his own teaching. What a teacher!

I explained to Andy that based on over two decades of study, psychologist Mihalyi Csikszentmihalyi, has coined the term, "flow," to refer to a state of concentrated action and awareness. A popular expression of this condition is "being in the zone." Research subjects describe flow as a state of being so engaged in an activity (e.g., running, writing, exploring, painting, dancing, performing, reading) that the senses of time, space, and outside stimuli are temporarily suspended. Respondents report that when they are in this depth of concentration, they feel energized and euphoric. They liken the feeling to being carried by a current, everything moving smoothly without effort. Csikszentmihalyi calls it flow—others call it fun.

> *Education is not the filling of a bucket, but the lighting of a fire.*
> – W. B. Yeats

My own conviction is that lifelong learning is not inspired by "teaching to the test," lock-step curriculum, or any other way of merely "filling the bucket." Master educators closely match the interests and abilities of students to fulfilling cognitive tasks. Thus, teachers help students learn the joy of the learning process rather than merely complying with preordained results. These "fire lighters" are able to motivate, invigorate, and empower students with activities so relevant and engaging that the learning process just seems to "flow." The mastery comes from being able to provide tasks that are challenging but still obtainable for students.

Lev Vygotsky (1978) defines this best possible set-up as one that is in the student's "zone of proximal development." The zone of proximal development is the distance between the student's present developmental level and the student's potential level of development (e.g. one that is reasonably attainable and yet just far enough beyond easy reach to sustain interest— somewhere between anxiety and boredom). Csikszentmihalyi agrees that when task requirements are high and personal skills are used to their fullest extent, learners are more likely to be absorbed in the process. Students become engaged, focused, and willing to keep pushing the limits of their abilities. Psychologists believe that when the learning experience gives this kind of intrinsic reward, students are far more likely to become self-propelled, self-motivated lifelong learners.

Promoting Flow in the Classroom

Csikszentmihalyi (1990) suggests basic guidelines for those who wish to promote flow in the classroom.

Teachers should:

- Be sensitive to students' goals and desires; use this knowledge to choose and frame activities that provide meaningful challenges.
- Empower students to take control of their own learning by giving them freedom within the context of clearly articulated goals.
- Provide clear and immediate feedback to students about how they are doing without making them feel inadequate or self-conscious.
- Arrange for students to have appropriate time to focus and help limit distractions.

Intuitive teachers observe when flow occurs naturally (such as a lively debate, writing in a journal, creating a multimedia presentation, playing a game, making and/or listening to music, or fashioning an art project) and learn to create similar experiences to engage students. They constantly monitor student activities and help them shift up or down depending on the difficulty of the task.

While the state of flow is an optimal learning situation for students, it is not something that normally occurs without *intentional* design by the teacher and *purposeful* effort by the learners. Experienced teachers make students aware that flow is something that requires work and responsibility on their part. They remind students that it was through deliberate practice and effort that Tiger Woods learned to swing a golf club, Britney Spears accomplished vocal timing and dance moves, and J. K. Rowling mastered the rules for syntax. Some drill and practice is often needed to make certain steps or movements so automatic that they no longer require conscious thought. This state of automaticity is needed in order to move on to higher levels of performance. Students more readily accept the repetitious tedium of learning basic skills when they are artfully blended with opportunities to engage in affirming states of flow.

Educators must find their own flow states in order to stay energized, excited, and effective in their work. Some school systems remain strongly entrenched in finding ways to select, organize, and distribute knowledge (filling the buckets), even though teachers know that paying attention to motivational issues (lighting the fires) is a more effective way to truly impact student learning. In short, filling the bucket is not effective because the results quickly evaporate. It is not an easy task, but the results of helping student open their gifts are permanent and add to the joy of learning for all involved. By validating and utilizing students' Multiple Intelligences and learning styles, teachers can be far more effective in achieving short-term and long-range educational goals with students. Thank you, Andy, and all the teachers who are out there lighting fires and drumming to the beat of their different marchers.

Recommended Reading List

Armstrong, Thomas. *Awakening Genius in the Classroom.* Alexandria, VA: Association for Supervision and Curriculum Development (ASCD), 1998.

Burke, Kay. *How to Assess Authentic Learning: The Mindful School.* Arlington Heights, IL: IRI/Skylight Publishing, Inc, 1999.

Campbell, Don. *The Mozart Effect: Tapping the Power of Music to Heal the Body, Strengthen the Mind, and Unlock the Creative Spirit.* NY: Avon Books, Inc, 1997.

Campbell, Linda and Bruce Campbell. *MIs and Student Achievement: Success Stories from Six Schools.* Alexandria, VA: Association for Supervision and Curriculum Development (ASCD), 1999.

Lazear, David G.. *Eight Ways of Knowing: Teaching for MIs.* Arlington Heights, IL: IRI/Skylight Publishing, Inc., 1999.

Tomlinson, Carol A. *How to Differentiate Instruction in Mixed-Ability Classrooms.* Alexandria, VA: Association for Supervision and Curriculum Development (ASCD), 2001.

CHAPTER 5

Cooperative Learning

Cooperative Learning or Chaos—
Is There Really a Difference?

Many years ago I was invited to address a teacher group about the benefits of using cooperative learning in the classroom. I explained the general concept of utilizing small groups of students engaged in specific learning tasks to achieve a common goal. One veteran teacher leaned back in his chair and announced to us all, "Yeah, we used to have that in my day, only back then it was called 'cheating'." We all laughed, but I could see he was serious.

I showed them the following picture on an overhead transparency for 20 seconds and asked the participants to memorize it:

I turned off the projector and asked each person to draw what she or he had seen. I admonished them not to cheat by talking to each other or by looking at each other's papers.

After about 3 minutes, most participants were very frustrated with their lack of ability to recall many of the details. I invited them to form groups of four and pool their memories to come up with a group picture. In every case the picture drawn by the four members had more detail and was more accurate that any of the individual renderings. When I asked the participants why this was so, they told me that the others had seen things they hadn't seen or hadn't remembered.

"Exactly," I responded. "That's one of the reasons businesses are moving towards more team work to accomplish goals and schools are using more cooperative learning."

Well-planned cooperative learning activities provide a complement to differentiated instruction. This inclusive teaching strategy emphasizes collaboration rather than competition and thus allows student to grow in self-esteem and academic achievement. Learning tasks are designed with different levels of complexity to challenge each child to learn something he or she did not know before; thus teachers can "raise the bar" for all. Individual contributions are enhanced and supported by feedback from the group. Group members' collected intelligences and styles allow students to capitalize on their own strengths while assisting others in areas where they are not so strong. In the process students learn about cooperation, equity, and the value of diversity.

What is Cooperative Learning?

Cooperative learning is an instructional strategy that utilizes small groups of students working together and helping one another on specific learning tasks with an emphasis on group members supporting one another.

Cooperative Learning is characterized by activities that:

1. **Require students to depend on one another for success.**
   Having students sit side by side working on something they could just as easily do by themselves is not cooperative learning.

Drumming to the Beat of a Different Marcher

Students must be required to share materials, knowledge, time, talents, and effort (or any combination of these).

2. **Provide for individual accountability.** Group members share jobs and make group presentations. Group members are tested individually and/or tested as a group to ensure that each person has mastered the required learning.

3. **Utilizes face-to-face interaction among students.** For all group work, students are arranged in close proximity of each other. They can be at tables, in desks or chairs pushed together, on the floor, or virtually anywhere they can do the task at hand separated from other groups.

4. **Focus on interpersonal and group skills**. Tasks are designed to include components of positive interpersonal communication skills such as active listening, building consensus, sharing, supporting, restating, using appropriate eye contact and gestures, and encouraging. Teams learn to stay on task and check each other for understanding.

Traditional Classroom	Cooperative Classroom
Learners are passive	Learners are active
Students work alone	Students work with 1 to 4 partners
Teacher directs work	Students direct work
Silence is valued	Learning noise is appropriate
Teacher initiates discussion	Students initiate discussion
Some students do not participate	All students participate
Individual accountability	Individual and group accountability
Independent learners	Interdependent learners
Affirmations come from teacher	Affirmations come from peers
Individual materials needed	Shared materials

Why Use Cooperative Learning?

The business world has repeatedly told us that the two most important skills we can foster in employees for the 21st century are (1) the ability to solve problems creatively and (2) the ability to work together to achieve a common goal. Our own school mission statements usually include references to students being caring members of the community and being non-judgmental towards others. Having students participate in various heterogeneous group arrangements is an exceptional way of getting them to talk to one another in a positive environment. Students with learning disabilities, poor language skills, physical impairment, and other challenges are able to get support from their peers as well as contribute to all group members' capacity for tolerance.

Purposeful cooperative learning activities help students develop interpersonal communication skills they will need later for marriage, jobs, families, friendships, and other social interactions. Intentional socialization components woven into learning activities help build a sense of community and common purpose for students. (Chapter 7 will address more about this emotional literacy consideration.)

Thirty years of research has shown that when cooperative learning used effectively, students achieve higher levels of thinking, retain more of what they learned, assume greater responsibility for their own learning, and have more affirmative feelings about school as well as the particular subject matter. Low-level, middle-level, and high-level learners demonstrate positive gains in cognitive transfer when cooperative learning is used as an instructional strategy.

Effective Use of Cooperative Learning Can:
- Increase achievement (at all ability levels)
- Empower students to take responsibility for their own learning
- Improve retention
- Generate more positive feelings towards the subject matter
- Provide more active learning
- Focus more time on learning
- Lower frustration and anxiety among students
- Enhance a sense of community among students
- Promote interpersonal communication skills
- Boost feelings of self-worth

How to Use Cooperative Learning

Early Childhood and Young Learners

At one time I believed that cooperative learning was an appropriate strategy for any student beyond the fourth grade. I hadn't considered using this strategy for younger children because my favorite model is a bit sophisticated for them. Often times when I worked with younger students they had so much difficulty with the process that they missed the content.

Then I began coaching lower elementary teachers who were using cooperative learning quite effectively. The secret was that they used a different model. Most of them introduced cooperative learning as a strategy between only two students. After the children mastered the techniques of working and sharing in twos the teachers sometimes grouped them in threes or more. Many times teachers assigned an activity for pairs and then had them combine with another set of pairs and so on until the group is as large as eight.

There are several successful models to aid lower elementary teachers of lower elementary students in developing strategies to illustrate positive social values and behaviors.

Foyle, Lyman, and Thies (1991) found that younger learners need:
- appropriate experiences (with modeling)
- adequate time
- opportunities to process the experience

Intermediate and Older Learners

With intermediate, middle level, and secondary learners I generally use groups of four or five. Depending on the time available, the difficulty of the task, the room arrangement, and the familiarity of the students with cooperative learning, the numbers of group members may vary. I generally stay away from groups larger than five because in most cases groups of six or more tend to break into subgroups, and it is difficult to create specific jobs for more than five. As with everything else I have suggested in this book, do whatever works best for your own situation.

In working with older learners it is important to remember that:

- Group members are responsible for the performance of each individual learner.
- Group members are individually accountable and must be able to report on or explain the team's results.
- The groups are to be assigned by the teacher. Their make-up should be heterogeneous with respect to sex, race, socioeconomic status, ability/learning styles, cliques, and other important factors.
- Leadership is shared on a rotating basis. Each team member has a job and responsibilities.
- The teacher is a resource; students are in charge of their own learning.
- Time must be allowed for group processing and self-evaluation.

The most common concerns cited by teachers for not using cooperative learning are:

1. The same students end up doing most or all of the work
2. Fear of losing control in the class
3. Difficulty in keeping students on track
4. Students who undermine the group success
5. Parents who complain/grades
6. Students in groups argue with one another
7. Takes up too much time
8. Materials get lost
9. Students work at different paces
10. Too much chaos

1. The same students end up doing most or all of the work.

In the model I prefer there are four to five jobs. The jobs rotate every time a new activity is assigned. Each student's seat has one of four colored dots (red, blue, yellow, or green) permanently stuck to it. On the wall are quarter-size posters with the name and responsibilities of each of the four jobs (see below). On each of the job posters there is a small Velcro™ tab at the bottom right edge. Stuck to the Velcro™ tab on the poster is a laminated circle (red, blue, yellow, or green) that has a Velcro™ tab glued to its back. At the beginning of the activity students look to see which job has a color dot to match the one on their seats. The matching dot is their job assignment for the lesson. I rotate the jobs by switching the circles on the posters before each activity to ensure that students have a chance to do all the jobs on an equal basis.

In front of each student is place a small laminated job placard. On the side that faces away from the student is the name of the job. On the side that faces the student is the list of the job responsibilities. These placards help remind the students of their jobs for the day and help me see if team members are doing their assigned tasks as I monitor the classroom.

The jobs I use are these:

Group Leader	Materials Manager
1. Reads all directions to group	1. Collects and returns all materials and supplies to appropriate place(s)
2. Leads discussions	2. Is the only one who can retrieve materials and supplies
3. Checks data sheet	3. Ensures everyone has equal access to materials and supplies
4. Helps with clean-up	4. Checks data sheet
5. Is the only one who can ask a question of the teacher	5. Helps with clean-up

Time Keeper	Data Collector
1. Holds team stopwatch (or watches the clock)	1. Collects data for activity
2. Keeps group on task and reminds them about time	2. Records data on appropriate form or sheet
3. Is responsible for getting the group to finish on time	3. Returns data sheet to teacher and/or records group data on class data sheet
4. Checks data sheet	4. Ensures all other team members check data sheet
5. Helps with clean-up	5. Helps with clean-up

Since this is not a perfect world, and all class populations are not divisible by four, I have a fifth job that can be assigned in a group:

Encourager

1. Monitors all team members to ensure they do their own jobs
2. Takes responsibility for praising and affirming jobs well done
3. Records comments and actions that show positive interpersonal communication
4. Reports recorded data to group at de-briefing session
5. Helps with clean-up

If a group of four has one member absent, two of the jobs can be combined for that day.

Part of the group's participation grade is based on how well each team member performs his or her job. Points are deducted if one team member does another team member's assigned responsibility. In this way each student is required to experience being the leader, being the person who writes the data, being the person who keeps others on task, and being the person who handles the materials. Since all team members must sign off on the completed data sheet (activity sheet, project report, etc.) everyone is involved in the process.

The fact that only the group leader can ask questions of the teacher keeps highly verbal students from always being the one to interact with the teacher. It is also helpful in restricting superfluous questions of the teacher since the team must discuss among themselves first before posing the problem to the teacher. Often they find the answer among themselves.

Since this model has no reporter job, students never know ahead who will be responsible for answering questions, making the report, or presenting the data. All team members must work together to ensure that everyone knows the material equally well. (I usually choose a color at random to assign the reporter for the activity.)

This model has been extremely successful for me in making sure that all students in each group participate, and no one student ends up doing all the work. I also monitor the groups as they work to ensure that everyone is doing his or her job. I take off points on the Group Participation Number Line (see #2) if one student is doing another student's job.

2. Fear of losing control in the class

The best way not to lose power is to give it away. Putting students in charge of their own learning is an extremely effective way of managing a class. What I find generally to be true is that teachers who do not ordinarily have classroom management problems with whole groups will not have management problems with small groups. Unfortunately, the opposite is also true. However, these tips can help with management issues:

- Have all materials ready and sorted before students arrive. Use paper box lids, plastic trays, or plastic tubs to hold necessary supplies

- Practice routines and procedures for cooperative learning before starting rigorously challenging graded assignments.

- Take it slowly. Prepare students for cooperative learning by doing team building activities first. Plan extra time for de-briefing social issues at the end of activities.

- Closely monitor groups and use the group participation number line to remind students about inappropriate behavior.

Group Participation Number Line

Date: _____ Group Number: _____

Group Members Present:

_____   _____

_____   _____

_____   _____

100 95 90 85 80 75 70 65 60 55 50 45 40 35 30 25 20 15 10 5 0

Participation Points Earned: _____

When the Materials Manager picks up the materials the Group Participation Number Line is with it. The Data Collector is to fill in the top 3 items and place the Number Line in an accessible place for the teacher. As the teacher monitors the groups, he or she will note any infractions of procedural or management standards by marking through the highest number not yet marked (100 is always first). At the end of the activity, the Data Collector (or the Encourager, if there is one) notes the highest number that is not marked through and enters it on the bottom line. This number represents the group's participation points.

The participation points are then averaged in with the activity score. The weight of the participation grade is up to the teacher. Participation may be 100% of the grade when doing introductory activities; later on it can be dropped to 50%, 25%, or lower. The teacher should be the judge of what works in terms of your short-term and long-range goals for their students.

3. Difficulty in keeping students on track

I have found two ways of keeping students focused. One is that I pay close attention as I monitor and mark off points on their Number Line for off-task behavior. More effective, however, is giving the students a set number of minutes to complete their tasks and having the Time Keeper keep up with the time. I purchase stopwatches just for this purpose. In lieu of stopwatches students can use their own watches or a classroom clock. Periodically as I am monitoring I say out loud,

"Time Keepers, watch your time." (Of course, occasionally you will have that concrete sequential student who takes his job too seriously. You will hear him telling his group, "We have 2 minutes and 55 seconds left . . . 54 . . . 53 . . . " I usually place a gentle hand on his shoulder and whisper, "Chill out, Son, you are working way too hard!")

4. Students who undermine the group success

One of the easiest solutions to handling a problem team member is to remove the student from the assigned group and make that person a group of one. Require him or her to do the same assignment in the same amount of time as the others. If the learning task has been structured in a true cooperative manner (and it always should be), the solitary student will be unable to produce a quality product alone and will suffer the penalty of reduced credit for the assignment. I have had students beg me to be put back on a group after this consequence.

A more proactive approach is to talk with individual students who seem to have difficulty relating to and cooperating with their peers. I once had a student, Doug, who was extremely intellectually gifted and had zero patience with those who were not as quick. At his worst he was extremely rude and stubborn. At his best he patronized and controlled the others. He openly stated that he did not want to be in anyone's group. When I put him in a group he would purposely try to get as many participation points taken off as he could to punish his teammates for ignoring him. No one wanted to have him in a group. In keeping with my focus on short-term and long-range goals, I considered Doug. I knew that he was very insecure about his peer relationships and that he used his superior intellect as a defense mechanism. I did not want him to continue to disrupt his groups and cause them to lose points. Doug had a lot to offer his peers, but he desperately needed some help with his relationships.

One day before I assigned new groups I asked three female students to join me in the hall. I believe in being up front with my students, and I told them the truth: "Girls, tomorrow I am going to assign new groups, and I am putting Doug in with you three."

They all groaned and rolled their eyes.

I said, "I know that Doug can be difficult. I have given this a lot of thought, and I tried to come up with the three most affirming, patient, compassionate students I know. You are the three that came to mind. I know it won't be easy, but Doug really needs someone to reach out to him, and I was thinking that you are the best three that can do it. Anytime you feel like you can't take it anymore, you can come and talk to me. I will support you every inch of the way. Personally, I think Doug is worth the effort. Will you give it a try?"

They all agreed. I placed Doug in their group and closely monitored their interactions. The girls did not let me down. They affirmed him, they were patient with him, and they encouraged him. Often one of them would wink at me when I walked by and they had Doug cooperating with them. Sometimes I would write each of them notes thanking them for their efforts. Soon Doug was working successfully with his group. I told Doug that I noticed how well he was doing with his new group. When it was time to assign new groups, I got a letter from the four asking if they could remain together for another round—they told me they wanted to keep their "family" together!

5. Parents who complain/grades

Like some teachers who really don't understand the true meaning of cooperative learning, many parents are confused. They believe cooperative learning will mean that some of the "not so smart" kids will pull down their child's grade or that their child will end up doing all the work.

The first thing I do is assure them that grades will come from a multitude of sources. I do grade cooperative learning activities, but I also grade independent projects, individual tests, individual assignments, portfolios, and alternative assessments. I inform them that, in general, cooperative activity grades are higher than individual scores. If they question a cooperative learning grade I always have the activity sheets that have been signed by each group member (including their own child).

If the complaint is about heterogeneous grouping, I am quick to tell parents that part of my job is to help students learn to get along with one another. I purposely design many of my class activities to teach and reinforce socialization skills. For parents of children identified as gifted who are afraid that the "lesser" children will slow their own child's progress, I show them the research that has proven all ability levels benefit from heterogeneous grouping. I explain to them about Multiple Intelligences and point out that students have strengths in different areas. One area that is notably lacking in many students identified as gifted is the interpersonal communication skill intelligence. Some of the highest suicide rates are among gifted students. I let them know that I see it as my responsibility to address the whole student by building a classroom community, and heterogeneous grouping is one way to facilitate that end.

6. Students in groups argue with one another

Teachers who do not take the time to practice procedures and routines for cooperative learning are asking for trouble. Unless students have had previous experience with effective cooperative learning practices, they are not likely to understand the expectations. It is well worth the teachers' time to purposefully go through the process with students at the beginning of the year. Fun activities can be used to acquaint students with rules and rituals.

In order to keep groups fresh and enthusiastic it is important to change them periodically. Younger students need a change more often. Older students can change groups every grading period. When our district went from 6-week to 9-week grading periods, I found that my sixth grade students needed to change groups more than 4 times during the year. I changed their groups every 4.5 weeks, and that seemed to work well. You will have to decide what is best in your case.

Just remember that every time you change groups, you have a different chemistry and a need for students to bond with their new teammates. Even after sharing several months in the same classroom, students have not been in the same exact groups. They still need to do one or two team-building activities before being assigned more intense academic tasks. This is one of my favorites.

Common Attributes

Once participants are arranged in groups, ask one member to be the recorder and write down each individual's name. A group leader should help the members discover 10 (hopefully unusual) common attributes. At the end of the ice breaker, one person from each group (chosen by the instructor) will introduce each group member and read their group's top 5 common attributes.

List each group member's name:

_____

_____

_____

_____

List your most unusual common attributes (they must be true and they must apply to ALL members of the group). When you are finished, put check marks (√) by your 5 favorite ones:

_____

_____

_____

_____

_____

_____

_____

_____

Drumming to the Beat of a Different Marcher
©2003 by Incentive Publications, Inc., Nashville, TN

Activities such as Common Attributes can be done as a competition. Older students can handle competitive cooperative group activities because they never have to lose alone. Building team spirit with a competitive emphasis such as a reward can also help allay student arguing. Ask your students for reward ideas. The following are some of my favorites:

Reward Ideas

Intermediate/Middle	Middle/High School
Line up for lunch first	Athletic event free pass
Bookmarks	Free test answer
Popcorn party	Free computer time
Snacks	Snacks
Free homework pass	Free homework pass
Stickers	First out of the classroom
Bonus points	Bonus points

7. Takes up too much time

Unfortunately a lot of teachers try cooperative learning only once or twice and are so concerned about the immense amount of time involved that they write it off as undoable. In the beginning stages of helping, students learn and practice the necessary steps, the going may be a bit slow. However, continued focus and training will eventually result in time saved. Because the teacher will be able to move freely about the room to clarify and re-teach without disturbing others, time will eventually be maximized.

It is true that a great deal of preparation time by the teacher is needed, but that is done before the students are present so class time is not lost. Students can be enlisted to clean-up and set-up for the next class so that teachers can actually save time usually spent managing materials.

8. Materials get lost

When teachers have their prized materials out in the classroom they sometimes worry that their "stuff" will get misplaced or removed. With the model I have presented there is very little chance of that happening. When the Materials Manager picks up the box lid, tray, or tub with the materials there is a list of everything that should be there. The MM checks to make sure that all materials and supplies are present before taking the items to the group. When the activity is over it is the responsibility of the MM to check to make sure that all the materials and supplies are back in place and to reset them for the next class. The MM immediately reports any missing or broken items to the teacher. (I once had an overzealous MM who wanted to do a strip search on his team members because of a missing magnet. I denied the request. We later found it stuck to a piece of metal on the underside of the table.)

9. Students work at different paces

Indeed, students do work at different paces, and so do groups. It is never a good idea to have students sitting idle waiting for others to finish.

Whether working with large groups, small groups, or individuals teachers always need to have supplementary activities ready for early finishers. For times when I want groups to work closer to the same speed, I do what I call "Directed Cooperative Learning." Students are given the complete set of written steps, but there are stop signs after certain sections. My instructions to the students are something like, "Go ahead and do Parts A & B and then work on the supplementary activity until I give you the go ahead." I then monitor the groups until most have finished the designated parts before I say, "I am now going to ask the students with green dots on their desks to share what your groups found." When we have thoroughly explored those parts, I say, "Now do Part C and stop. If you have extra time you can begin filling out your activity log." And so on. By directing students to do certain parts and stop, I am better able to informally assess as we go along and adjust my teaching accordingly.

10. Too much chaos

There is nothing chaotic about cooperative learning that is well-planned and well-managed. Teachers should plan activities that are challenging and yet doable if the group members work together. Tasks should require the concentrated efforts of all team members doing their jobs and working within the allotted time. Materials and supplies should be out and sorted before students arrive. During the cooperative learning activity it is the responsibility of the teacher to monitor the students and:

- Give immediate feedback and reinforcement for learning

- Re-teach certain concepts if necessary

- Clarify directions

- Encourage oral elaboration

- Affirm positive interactions and efforts

- Informally assess student learning and collaboration

Another way to ensure that the cooperative learning activity is organized and has a smooth closure is to allow time after clean-up and whole group information sharing to ask the groups to evaluate how they interacted with one another. Either verbally (or in their journals) students can answer questions like these:

- Tell how involved each of your team members was in the decisions your group made.

- How do you feel about the work your group did today? Why?

- What would you would like to tell your teammates about how you felt during today's activity or the way you feel now?

- What could your team do to improve the way you get along and/or work together?

- What is your favorite thing about being on this team?

Teachers need to keep a close watch on the personal interactions going on within groups. Happy well-functioning groups matched with appropriate tasks and given adequate time constraints run smoothly.

Helping Students with Socialization

As a teacher gains more experience, he or she will learn to do more than one thing at a time. A sponge activity designed to engage students as they walk in the door will be revisited as a learning activity sometime during the class period. A cooperative learning activity can be used to reinforce social skills while also working on content knowledge.

Whenever I can I give students a socialization skill to work on in their groups along with whatever cognitive task I have assigned. For instance, when students are first assigned to their groups I tell them that I will be tallying the number of times I hear them use each other's correct first names. As I monitor I carry a clipboard and keep a tally for each group. After all the debriefing on the activity I announce the winning group and give a small prize.

Other socialization skills that I reinforce this way are:

- rephrasing what a teammate says before making your own statement
- positively affirming and encouraging one another
- taking turns
- sharing materials
- listening attentively to one another
- building consensus

Alternative Ways to Use Cooperative Learning

1. Within a lecture or presentation:
   The teacher is discussing, modeling, or explaining something. He or she pauses to ask small groups to summarize, categorize, debate, describe, or otherwise react to the presented material.

2. With higher level questioning:
   The teacher asks small groups to come up with a team consensus on something to do with analysis, synthesis, or evaluation of the concept being discussed.

3. As practice reinforcement:
   The teacher asks students to get with their groups to practice, memorize, or review the given concepts.

4. Decision-making/problem solving:
   The group is to reach a decision or solve a problem presented by the teacher. For example, the teacher is leading a class discussion on the separation of church and state in the United States Constitution. She asks small groups to meet and decide whether or not to include the words, "Under God" in the Pledge of Allegiance. Groups are to figure out a way for students to say the Pledge without violating the spirit of the law.

5. As a review:
   The teacher asks a question. Team members put their heads together to discuss the answer. The teacher calls out a color, and the person who has that color dot will answer the question as the teacher whips through the groups.

6. In a tournament or game format:
   There are several models for using cooperative learning in a tournament or game format. Student Teams-Achievement Divisions (STAD) and Teams-Games-Tournament (TGT) are two of the more popular ones.

7. With peer editing:
   Team members proofread each other's work and offer suggestions
   for improvement. This practice helps both the "corrector" and
   the "correctee."

8. As an assessment:
   A Gallery Walk (sometimes called Carousel Walk) is a way to assess
   students in groups. The teacher puts large pieces of newsprint around
   the room. On the top of each is a question for which there are several
   answers. Student groups are given different colored markers and asked
   to write one correct answer to each question. Answers cannot be
   repeated on a page. The teacher can informally assess student learning
   by listening to them as they "think out loud" in their groups (Slavin
   calls this oral elaboration). Or teachers can more formally assess the
   answers by noting the flow of answers used by each colored group.

9. Research projects or group investigations:
   Group work on projects can promote sharing of the load and
   commitment to a time line. Often students who are procrastinators
   when it comes to doing their own work will get motivated by their
   peers to finish their part of the assignment.

10. Checking homework:
    Even though homework is for independent practice, many teachers
    have limited time for checking and correcting it during a rushed day.
    Group members can check each other's work for accuracy.

For more information on the specific techniques mentioned in this
chapter or for lessons designed around particular age groups and subject
areas consult your local bookstore or the Internet. Cooperative learning
strategies abound. Using small group interactions is a powerful teaching tool
that can be used to enhance the learning cycle and most other effective
teaching strategies. Different marchers hearing different songs still need to
learn to work successfully in groups when the need arises. Learning
interpersonal communication skills helps students to become better citizens.
Working in groups helps students "get better together."

Recommended Reading List

Johnson, David, et al. *The New Circles of Learning: Cooperation in the Classroom and School.* Alexandria, VA: Association for Supervision and Curriculum Development (ASCD), 1994.

Foyle, Harvey C., et al. *Cooperative Learning in the Early Childhood Classroom.* Np: National Education Association, 1994.

Slavin, Robert E. *Cooperative Learning: Theory, Research, and Practice.* Englewood Cliffs, NJ: Prentice Hall, 1990.

CHAPTER 6

Utilizing Technology

Is It Using Technology
If I Set My Laser Pointer to Stun?

> *I have a spelling checker; it came with my PC.*
> *It clearly marks four my revue miss steaks I cannot sea;*
> *I ran this poem threw it. I'm your please to no.*
> *Its let her perfect in it's weight, my checker tolled me sew.*
>
> — Arthur Unknown (Holdstein, 1994, p. 9)

Learning about Technology

I was very fortunate in that I was brought into the technological world by my friend, mentor, and computer guru, Jerry Antee. I have never met a more gifted, patient computer coach. I was the most inept person in our class, and I would constantly lament to him that I felt so foolish because I didn't know half of what the other teachers in the course knew. Jerry said to me, "You know, the only reason you don't already know this is because you didn't have a reason to know it before. Now you do, so you will learn it." And I did!

Anyone wanting to learn about technology should search for an instructor who is understanding, kind, and will make a student do things independently. It also helps if the person teaching has a learning style that works for the learner. Teachers may find that their best technology instructor is one of their students.

Without a doubt, technology has improved the quality of my work. Learning how to make really nice handouts for students, to use some of the new science probeware, to make concept maps with software, and to use spreadsheets to reduce my endless bookkeeping was such a boost! When I learned how to search the Internet for new lesson plan ideas and resource materials, it reignited my passion for teaching science. I have heard several teachers say that new technology available to teachers and students has renewed their excitement for teaching as well.

One thing to remember is not to be afraid of the new technology. In most cases it cannot be damaged that badly, so find out the safety issues and then start "messing with it." The best way to learn about technology is to use technology. Play with and practice using new technological tools on a regular basis. Take (or make) the opportunity to go to workshops, conferences, and seminars for technology. There will be true "techies" there who generally love to help those who are eager to learn! Don't be self-conscious.

JOKE:
Oh-no-second: the time between when you've hit "enter" and you realize what you've done!

Using Technology to Improve Instruction

ISTE National Educational Technology Standard (NETS) and Performance Indicators for Teachers

I. Technology Operating Concepts

II. Planning and Designing Learning Environments and Experiences

III. Teaching, Learning, and the Curriculum

IV. Assessment and Evaluation

V. Productivity and Professional Practice

VI. Social, Ethical, Legal, and Human Issues

The Internet has a wealth of ideas for teachers. When using a search engine, type in the grade level, area of discipline, and subject topic. Attaching the words "lesson plans" "learning cycle" or "hands-on" will yield a wealth of ideas to help in reforming teaching practices. Other fairly common technologies that can be very useful in general are:

- Word processing programs
- Databases/Spreadsheets
- Outlining
- Desktop Publishing
- Graphics
- Audio and Video Capturing

- Authoring software
- Online Mentoring
- Whiteboards
- Chatrooms
- Portable keyboards

Other Uses of Technology

- Many health and P.E. teachers are using heart monitors and motion software.

- Special needs students can be helped immensely with special adaptive devices.

- Reaching out to parents, posting student work, emailing experts or other students. Limitless potential.

- Digital cameras give instant affirmation as well as tremendous power with groups.

- Art is making a comeback because of multimedia programs. New job market for web designers and other multimedia artists including video and music software.

- Multimedia tools can engage heretofore unengaged students who are attracted to the "bells and whistles," which is fine as long as they learn something in the process.

- For children with language deficits, software programs are available. Dyslexic students can get visual and auditory support from computer programs.

Tips for Teaching with Technology

- Be careful that the medium does not overwhelm the message.

- Always protect a child's privacy online.

- Teach student proper online etiquette.

- Be discriminating in your site selections. The Web is overrun with advertisements and uneven in quality.

- Invest in technology for your home or arrange with your school to "check out" things to take home and practice.

- For students who have no access to either the Internet or a computer at home, suggest other accesses (e.g. school facilities, public library).

- Put students on computers in pairs or in threes. They do much better.

- If you serve on technology committees always ask yourself, "Who is piloting this ship?" Technology should support instruction, not the other way around (oftentimes hardware and software representatives try to dictate what your curriculum should look like so that they can sell a product.)

- If you incorporate technology into your lesson, have a back-up plan.

- Use technology to enhance and invigorate learning. Simply reading slides to students is boring!

- Don't be afraid of it. It's not that fragile. Really. (Remember: it all boils down to 1's and 0's).

Alternative Assessment through Technology

Technology can also add a new component to student assessment. Like viewing a movie scene from different camera angles to enlarge perspective, technology can broaden the view and help illuminate demonstrated capability.

Computer data and video clips help teachers keep records and look deeper for student understanding. Electronic student portfolios in which students select what is collected adds another dimension to their assessment. For more information see Helen Barnett's "Technology Support for Alternative Assessment" http://transition.alaska.edu/www/portfolio/TechPort1.html

Ideas for Alternative Assessment with Technology

Technology that is available in most schools can be utilized to assess students as well as to inspire Higher-Order thinking. Consider these examples:

Image Editing Software
Higher-Order Thinking (synthesis, evaluation)
Example: Create a collage of pictures that portray influences of multiculturalism in this community.

Video
Higher-Order Thinking (application, analysis, synthesis, evaluation)
Example: Create a video that demonstrates how to apply the scientific method to problem-solving.

> *Any sufficiently advanced technology is indistinguishable from magic.*
> – Arthur C. Clarke

Power Point

Higher-Order Thinking (application, synthesis, evaluation)

Example: Create a presentation that shows how the United States might be different if the South had won the Civil War.

Web Page

Higher-Order Thinking
(application, analysis, synthesis, evaluation)

Example: Create a web page that teaches younger students about the importance of making good health choices.

Hyperstudio

Higher-Order Thinking
(application, analysis, synthesis, evaluation)

Example: Create a virtual tour of the digestive system.

Spreadsheet Program

Higher-Order Thinking
(application, analysis, synthesis, evaluation)

Example: Use real data to graph and analyze the average jumps of 5 students who

(a) jump with knees locked and arms straight to the side
(b) jump with knees locked and arms allowed to swing freely
(c) jump with knees bent and arms locked to the side
(d) jump with knees bent and arms allowed to swing freely

Give an explanation for the results.

Other Cautions about Using Technology

Do not become overzealous in the use of technology just because it is new. Don't use technology simply for technology's sake. After all, one could argue that at one time pencils and paper were a technological break-through.

The machinery is here, but we are still exploring how best to use them to enhance student learning. Whether it be through the use of automation of traditional models of teaching, enabling new models of teaching and learning, or extending teaching and learning beyond the walls of the school, technology is fundamentally a tool of teaching and should be used to support learning. Teachers must be able to utilize technology-based learning environments to enhance their instructional and assessment strategies. Through technology they can help students better communicate, explore, and learn. In all cases, technology must support learning. Technology integration is the wrong approach. Think about how technology can be a tool to extend and support what is being taught.

Jane M. Healy (1998), author of *Failure to Connect: How Computers Affect Our Children's Minds—for Better and Worse* agrees that it is superfluous to use technology for what can be done more easily and better with paper, pencil, and a human teacher. She says that we may find eventually that some courses (e.g. high school English) are better taught without technology. Educators have to be the final judge of what is appropriate and what is not.

Even the most ardent techies in the world know that technology cannot replace good teachers. Technology is a tool. It's not about the gadgets, the RAM, or the best toys—it's about educators. It's about educators knowing their subjects inside and out. It's about knowing students. It's about going in after them with whatever it takes. Sometimes technology can help a teacher do a better job of that, so I am thankful that we have it. I am worried when it has us. Always remember that the computer is an inadequate substitute for human intelligence.

> *In a time of drastic change it is the learners who inherit the future. The learned usually find themselves equipped to live in a world that no longer exists.*
>
> – Eric Hoffer

Recommended Reading List

Hopkins, Tim. *1001 Best Websites for Educators.* Westminster, CA: Teacher Created Materials, Inc., 2000.

Jukes, Ian. *Windows on the Future: Education in the Age of Technology.* Thousand Oaks, CA: Corwin Press, Inc., 2000.

Recommended Web Sites

Bilingual Books for Kids
bilingualbooks.com/

Children's Literature Web Guide
ucalgary.ca/~dkbrown/

Kathy Schrock's Guide for Educators
school.discovery.com/schrockguide

Learning Through Collaborative Visualization
(science instruction)
covis.nwu.edu

Consortium for School Networking
cosn.org/

Tammy's Technology Tips for Teachers
essdack.org/tips

The Committed Sardine
thecommittedsardine.net

The International Society for Technology in Education(ISTE)
iste.org

INTRODUCTION TO PART THREE

Stepping to Your Own Music
(Pulling It All Together)

It is not always easy to merge your own mission with the agendas of others. This section addresses the occasional dissonance between the cognitive and the affective domains in education. It speaks openly about everyday issues that affect teachers and offers suggestions on how they can teach to standards without losing a part of themselves in the process.

In Chapter 7 the concept of emotional literacy is clarified and examined. Methods for integrating interpersonal and intra-personal skills within the curriculum are offered.

Chapter 8 explains the importance of and gives examples for what is meant by "the heart of teaching."

PART 3
Stepping to Your Own Music (Pulling It All Together)

Chapter 7 Building a Classroom Community
Emotionally Literate Educators? Not An Oxymoron!

Chapter 8 Pay It Forward
*But I'm Not Even Through Paying Back
My Student Loans!*

Building A Classroom Community

Emotionally Literate Educators?
Not An Oxymoron!

> *"If facts are the seeds that later produce knowledge and wisdom, then the emotions and the impressions of the senses are the fertile soil in which the seeds must grow."*
> — Rachel Carson

The Sense of Wonder

Where Have All the Children Gone?

Sometimes I look around at the overly made-up, skin-baring, trouser-bagging, flesh-pierced, hip-hopping, too-cool-for-words young people today, and I am saddened by their lost childhood. Some of our students appear to have missed the fundamental delight in just "being kids." Their behavior often comes across as tasteless and without manners.

If adults wonder why children today seem to be acting poorly, they should try doing a little culture check. Watch the television programs they view on a regular basis. Most of the comedy they watch models laughter that comes at the expense of someone else. Listen to the words to their music; validation of violent acts, low tolerance, and disrespect are the norm. Check out the video games they are playing. Children are invited to kill and maim simulated people to win points. It's a little scary out there. Certainly there are some positive programs, inspiring songs, and relatively harmless video games for children, but they are by far less popular than the aforementioned ones.

Today's headlines scream of man's inhumanity to man. Everywhere there is news of corporate thieves, unethical politicians, and flawed heroes. Our children are constantly barraged with negative examples of adult conduct.

Pair the lack of appropriate role models with the breakdown of the traditional family, and it is easy to see why children today seem so conflicted. Parents are working harder and longer to provide the kids with material things, but they are home a reduced amount of time, less attentive when they are there, and infrequently share an uninterrupted family meal with their offspring. For some families, most all of their traditional rituals are a thing of the past. In short, today's children have lost something important—a connection to families, to a shared history, and to each other.

Those who were born before 1965 can probably remember a now virtually extinct category of clothing called play clothes. Children of that time arrived home from school and changed into play clothes. This made sense because these children usually had a large chunk of unencumbered time available to just go outside and seriously play. They interacted with their siblings, neighbors, and friends in games that were not highly organized and required no special equipment. There were no uniforms, no referees, and no Title IX compliance regulations. Kids just played. A lot of socialization took place during this playtime. Children learned to get along, to cooperate, and to handle themselves.

Today's children don't have play clothes because generally they don't go out and play. Some children cannot go out and play because it is no longer safe for children to be outside unsupervised. Some children cannot go out and play because they are so over-scheduled into extracurricular lessons and activities that there is no time left for fun. And still some choose not to go out and play because they would rather interact with a computer or sit passively in the presence of a TV or CD player than actually get up and do something. It's not my intent to comment on America's pop culture here, but I do want to make one point: Today's children are missing an important socialization process, and schools are suffering because of it.

This chapter is about addressing the lack of socialization and feelings of self-efficacy in our students. It is written to help teachers build a caring community in their classrooms. The basis for this chapter is the time-honored belief that in order for children to learn they must first feel safe and secure. It capitalizes on new evidence about the relationship between cognitive transfer and emotions. It also focuses on the need for teachers to address directly and indirectly the components of social learning.

The education community fully acknowledges that when students come to school unable to read, it is our responsibility to teach them to read. Likewise, when pupils struggle with math, it is our duty to teach them how to compute numbers and solve problems. But what about the children who come to us who don't know how to act appropriately, or whose job is it to deal with that particular deficiency? My belief is that the answer is "everyone's job." Some students have more highly developed "people skills" and resiliency than others, but all students can benefit from a curriculum rich with opportunities to hone their interpersonal communication and their intra-personal awareness competencies (social learning).

Typical classroom exchange at Bangyerhead Ondewall Middle School:

The teacher notices a young lady crying and asks, "Charlotte, what is wrong?"

Charlotte replies, "Bryan told me my new braces make me look like a geek."

The teacher says to Charlotte, "Well, you don't look like a geek, so just ignore what he says and take out your book." Charlotte continues to cry.

The teacher is annoyed with Bryan and turns to him, "Why would you say a thing like that to Charlotte? I thought she was your friend."

Bryan shrugs, "I was just kidding with her."

The teacher says, "Bryan, how can you call that kidding? What you said to Charlotte hurt her. Haven't you noticed how self-conscious she has been today because she has those new braces on her teeth?"

Bryan answers defensively, "No, I didn't know anything was wrong with her."

The teacher says, "Well, she has been hiding her mouth and ducking her head all morning. How could you have missed that?"

Bryan looks astonished. "I didn't see her do that!"

The teacher gets aggravated. "Bryan, you couldn't have missed it. You're a very bright young man. Now don't sit there and tell me that you didn't know Charlotte was already upset about her new braces."

Bryan is now getting mad. "Well, I didn't! And I don't know what the big deal is, anyway. Lots of people have braces. She won't have to wear them for life or anything! I can't help it if she's going to try and get me in trouble for just kidding her. Just forget it. I don't like her anyway. I'm always the one who gets in trouble for stuff I didn't even do. I hate this class and everybody in it!"

And so it goes . . .

The really sad part about this encounter is that Bryan is telling the truth. He is totally bewildered about Charlotte's response and the teacher's censure. He really doesn't have a clue as to what all the fuss is about. Even though his achievement test scores are among the top in his class, Bryan is socially obtuse. He isn't what Howard Gardner refers to as "people smart." He doesn't know how to read body language or pick up on visual clues from others. He is unable to put himself in Charlotte's position and discern what she is feeling. He is unwilling to take any personal responsibility for the situation, and he would rather give up on the friendship than try to work it out. In the end, he lets his own emotions get out of hand, and he overreacts to the situation. Bryan lacks emotional intelligence.

Neither Charlotte nor Bryan is likely to learn any of the information about verb conjugation that the teacher is getting ready to present. Both are upset by the disturbing confrontation that just took place. At best the teacher can try to quiet the two of them so that the rest of the students can get back on task, but those two students have lost this period of learning time.

Is there anything that can be done to prevent or at least minimize situations like this? What happens to instructional time when teachers constantly have to troubleshoot disputes and off-task behavior?

I actually had an education professor once tell me that a good lesson plan will take care of any behavior problems in a classroom. (Yeah, right. And a well-planned highway system takes care of all your traffic woes.) While good lesson plans are absolutely essential, anytime people are involved unexpected things always happen—in life and at school as well. Because classrooms are filled with young humans who have unique sets of experiences, expectations, and emotional intelligences (and in middle school you have to throw in that hormone thing) their precise reactions and interactions cannot be predicted, planned, or controlled. (That's what keeps it fun!)

Teachers can act proactively to build a sense of community in the class that will help smooth the way through most daily occurrences.

She or he can also put into place methods for handling unexpected events. The key is that a safe and caring classroom community must be shaped *from the beginning*. Teachers must work purposefully with students individually and with the group collectively to develop their emotional literacy.

In the past, when teachers took time out to work on activities designed to build harmony in the classroom, they were told that it is best just to "stick to the subject matter." They were admonished not to "waste" valuable class time dealing with affective issues. Nevertheless, they persevered with attempts to build unity and a cooperative spirit in their classes because it was their experience that spending the time deliberately focused on strengthening the affective side of classes eventually paid off in more time on task and greater learning. They weren't sure why some students seemed to be natural leaders or peacemakers, but they realized that all children did not have the same abilities for working together or even for working independently.

Before we had Howard Gardner to help us identify student intelligences, we often said that those who had the interpersonal communication intelligence had the "gift of gab" (actually my own teachers called my "gift" a "curse"!), and those who didn't have it were dismissed as excessively shy or social misfits. We said that those who had the intra-personal awareness intelligence were self-actualized and self-motivated, and those who didn't have it were immature or had an inferiority complex. We relied on Abraham Maslow to help us work through the requisite stages for helping our students feel self-fulfilled, but we seldom got past #3.

Maslow's Need Hierarchy (1954)
1. Physiological needs: food, drink, sex, and shelter.
2. Safety needs: security, order, protection, and family stability.
3. Love needs: affection, group affiliation, and personal acceptance.
4. Esteem needs: self-respect, prestige, reputation, and social status.
5. Self-actualization needs: self-fulfillment and achievement of personal goals, ambitions, and talent.

Drumming to the Beat of a Different Marcher

Then along came a *New York Times* reporter, Daniel Goleman, who became interested in his and others' observations that the most successful people were often not those with the highest intelligence quotients (I.Q.'s). He read research on emotional intelligence (E.I.) done by Peter Salovey at Yale University and John Mayer at the University of New Hampshire that indicated I.Q. was actually a very poor determiner of eventual success. Mr. Goleman interviewed researchers and psychologists across America, then wrote a groundbreaking book on E.I. In his research on American students, Goleman found that there is a noticeable decline in social skills that traverses all socio-economic, racial, and gender lines.

What is E.I.?

Classroom teachers do not need to be told us that there is more violence, less student motivation, and more so-called behavior disorders than ever before in our schools. Most of us have witnessed a greater number of children who feel sad, bewildered, lonely, confused, and anxious. Student remarks to one another as well as to the adults in the school are more tactless and insensitive than ever before. There seems to be an increasing number of children who have trouble recognizing dangerous situations and who persist in actions they know will get them into trouble. We are gratified, however, that Mr. Goleman has validated the importance of addressing emotions in all areas of life including schools.

In a 1996 interview with John O'Neil, Goleman elaborated on the E.I. concept. "Emotional intelligence is a different way of being smart. It includes knowing what your feelings are and using your feelings to make good decisions in life. It's being motivated and remaining hopeful and optimistic when you have setbacks in working towards goals. It's empathy; knowing what the people around you are feeling. And it's social skill—getting along well with other people, managing emotions in relationships, being able to persuade or lead others."

Goleman goes on to state that at best one's life accomplishments are only about 20 percent attributable to I.Q. People who possess a high I.Q. are not necessarily ethical, moral, kind, good partners, competent parents, or valuable contributors to society. On the other hand, people with high E.I. are, in general, happier, more successful, and more socially responsible. As a rule they experience more job satisfaction and harmony in their lives and have less addiction problems. Goleman believes, and many educational researchers concur, that emotional intelligence is at least as important if not more important than I.Q.for impacting a person's ultimate success.

While Harvard psychologist Jerome Kagan (1994) believes that the first 24 months of a child's life provide a dramatic impact on how the child will turn out emotionally, his research clearly demonstrates that E.I. can be taught and learned from childhood through adolescence. Many believe that a neurological window of opportunity for emotional centers in the brain extends into the teens. This is heartening news for educators. We now know that teachers can play an intentional role in helping students master the social and emotional skills they need.

In today's students, there exists a sometimes hidden abuse—the killing of a child's spirit. Children who have not been nurtured or valued understandably often lack resiliency and social skills. The good news is that schools can frequently reverse the effects of emotional deficits. By incorporating deliberate procedures and activities that promote the people smart and self-smart levels of intelligence in all students, educators can provide emotionally safe classrooms for all.

> *The most deadly of all sins is the mutilation of a child's spirit.*
> – Erik H. Erikson

The Essential Elements of E.I.
- Knowing one's emotions
- Managing emotions
- Motivating oneself
- Recognizing emotions in others
- Handling relationships

Salovey (as quoted in Goleman, 1995)

Why is Emotional Intelligence Important?

In the last decade, the emergence of new brain research has given us more than enough data to support our intuitive belief that cognition and emotion go hand in hand. Learning environments that encourage trust, creativity, spontaneity, wonder and joy contribute to more motivated students. Research shows that schools that have emotional literacy programs in place (sometimes called character education) have students who are better behaved, pay better attention, and need less discipline. Policymakers should note that achievement scores in these same schools tend to be higher, too.

These findings are not surprising. Common sense tells us that students need to remain hopeful and motivated in order for learning to occur. It is obvious that students who are chronically anxious, angry, or otherwise upset cannot keep their minds off the things they are worried about. Their memory centers have limited attention capacity, and emotional needs get first priority.

Eric Jensen (1998) maintains that emotions drive attention, meaning, and memory. He also believes they play an important part in the decision-making process. He reports that E.I. has finally received the attention it deserves because of three recent discoveries in the field of neuroscience:

1. The discovery of the physical pathways and priorities of emotions.

2. Findings that the brain's chemicals are involved in emotions.

3. A discovered link between the pathways and chemicals to learning and memory.

He and others in the educational field now believe there are scientific reasons to explain why it is that when children feel safe their minds expand, tolerance is enhanced, conversations are improved, and more connections are made.

Not since John Dewey urged educators in 1916 to teach "the whole child" has there been such a promising call to action. It has always been the teacher's challenge to create a classroom that focuses on students' social, ethical, and intellectual development. Finally, there is definitive research to support that goal.

Knowing One's Emotions

> *"The child must first learn self-respect and a sense of dignity that grows out of his increasing self-understanding before he can learn to respect the personalities and rights and differences of other."*
> —Virginia M. Axline

In order for a person to effectively manage emotions, he or she must first be aware of them. Many students have been taught to ignore feelings. When I was growing up my mother often said to me, "Stop crying, or I'll give you something to cry about!"

Over and over children are told that their feelings are not valid: "You do *not* hate your little brother! Don't you ever say that again," or "Yes, you *do*, too, like to go to church. Now act like it!" No wonder students come to school questioning their own feelings!

Here's a very simple truth that a counselor once told me about feelings: They Are. That's it—two words, feelings are. No one has the right to tell another person how she or he feels. It is important to let students know that they alone have the power to change their feelings by altering their thoughts. Whether or not they choose to reveal their feelings is up to them, but it is crucial that they learn to acknowledge their true feelings at least to themselves.

Reading trade books in which characters freely express their own feelings can help start discussions about self-understanding. Students can also be taught to monitor their physical reactions such as rapid heartbeat, welling tears, tightened throat, constricted breathing, sweating, and stomach pains for cues to their true emotions.

Once students learn to acknowledge what they are experiencing, they can decide how to express it and deal with it. Journaling, drawing, dancing, singing, writing, sculpting, talking, and role-playing are just a few of the acceptable ways for students to express their feelings. (Personally, I like to mount large photos of a certain school superintendent on watermelons and drop them from high places, but I don't recommend that to children.) Being able to label a feeling is the first step to being able to diminish its power over them. They should be made aware that feeling an emotion does not mean that they are awful people (i.e. "Right now I hate my best friend, so I must be a terrible human being."). Eventually students can learn to change their thinking patterns in order to master their feelings.

Nagy and Nagy (1999) advise that we teach students to recognize the "deepest truth about themselves." In other words, we must constantly give them opportunities to be reminded that they are fundamentally kind, loving, and lovable human beings. When children feel guilty for their negative emotions, it is important that they learn to say to themselves: "I am not a terrible human being who hates my best friend. I am a good person who feels angry right now because she didn't pick me for the team. I need to remind myself about the things I value in my friend so that I can reframe my reaction to this situation."

An activity that works with acknowledging emotions as well as the other essential components of E.I. is "From the Heart." It is one of my all-time favorite class activities because it can be used in so many different situations such as after a tragedy, a theft/act of vandalism, a divisive circumstance, an unfair competition, or any number of upsetting events that happen to students. It is important when fostering a caring culture in the classroom that teachers are open, honest, and frank with students. Likewise, teachers should encourage students to be direct as well as tactful.

From the Heart

Materials:

Stuffed animal or plush heart cushion

Set-up:

Participants should be seated in a circle. The leader should also be in the circle.

Purpose:

The purpose of this activity is to facilitate communication among students, staff, and others who need to work together. Participants communicate their own feelings and listen to the feelings of others. Cooperation is reinforced through the sharing of individual feelings and the practice of listening skills.

Procedure:

The leader sits with students in a circle (either on the floor or in chairs). One at a time, participants share their feelings or ideas on a topic while holding the stuffed toy. When the student is finished, he or she passes the stuffed animal on to the next person. This continues until everyone has had the opportunity to share. The leader also shares but is careful not to dominate the activity.

Subjects:

Generally it is best to start students with "safe" subjects such as: . . .
– I like it when . . .
– My favorite thing to do is . . .
– My favorite quality in a person is . . .
– I am happy when . . .

Subjects of more depth can be explored once participants build trust among one another and become more comfortable with the activity.

Ground Rules:

1. Only the participant with the stuffed toy may talk. Everyone else actively listens and supports the person who is speaking.

2. A participant ALWAYS has the right to pass and give the animal to the next person.

3. Anything shared in this activity is PRIVATE! Participants should be aware that nothing communicated during "From The Heart" should be told outside the group. Everything must be held in confidence.

4. No one participant should monopolize the activity. Students should be sure that everyone gets a turn.

5. Participants should talk only about what they feel, not about how others in the group feel.

6. The stuffed toy should be handled and passed gently.

7. The leader should also share.

Additional Information:

"From the Heart" is a safe, simple way of sharing feelings. It is effective with ALL students, whether shy or demanding of attention. Teachers who use "From the Heart" report that students exhibit:
– calmness and less anxiety
– more overall participation and productivity

"From the Heart" is an activity that can be used to help students through difficult situations, such as:
– death of a class pet
– accident or death of a student or staff member
– a fight
– a team loss
– an embarrassing moment
– a theft
– a disappointment

> *We must structure opportunities into each child's daily routine that will enable him or her experience feelings of competence, belonging, usefulness, potency, and optimism.*
>
> – Sagor, 1996.

Managing Emotions

Just like Bryan (in the scenario with Charlotte) let his emotions spin out of control, students sometimes let their feelings control their behavior. One of the advantages to acknowledging feelings for what they are is that it enables us to control them rather than the other way around. Extreme emotions are seldom conducive to learning goals. Hurtful or violent actions are never acceptable. Students can be taught to handle their feelings appropriately through modeling, role-play, writing assignments, reading assignments, and discussions.

Brainstorm with students about examples of individuals who let their emotions overcome good judgment (road rage, students involved in school violence, and/or examples suitable to their grade level and experience). Ask them to generate a list of alternative choices that would be more fitting. Stress to students that while feelings "are," what we do about our feelings is a matter of choice—always. Remind them that while they may not like any of the choices they have, they can at least pick the least unpleasant one and start to work on it. Learning to manage their emotions is empowering to students and acts to help build their overall self-esteem.

Low E.I. students often are unable to delay actions or gratification. A coping mechanism for those who are trying to control their feelings (and/or impulsivity) is to learn to anchor themselves to something pleasing or calming. Much like repeating a positive mantra during meditation, students can learn to visualize a pleasing scene, "play" a soothing melody in their minds, or use whatever coping mechanism that works for them. Provide students with a "time-out" to regain composure. Counting to ten may not be all that helpful; psychologists now say that a more reasonable time period for calming down is between 15 to 20 minutes. (When dealing with officious bureaucrats it usually takes me between 15 to 20 hours to calm down!) Educators must consistently remind students that while they cannot control all situations, they can always control their reactions to them. Help students practice staying calm no matter what is going on around them. (Teachers sometimes need the practice, too!).

Drumming to the Beat of a Different Marcher

Students with low E.I. tend to feel a need to assign blame to others. They need help in reframing events. "Reframing" is a term that means to try and look at something from another perspective. Just as reframing a picture with different types and colors of frames will make the image seem to change, thinking about a situation from other viewpoints can alter perspective and feelings. In the situation where the child is upset that her best friend did not pick her to be on her team, she could first remember what she values in her friend and then try to see the action from a different viewpoint:

"My best friend really worries about other people's feelings. Perhaps she was trying to pick some of the less popular kids for her team and was counting on me to understand."

-or-

"My friend has a very strong sense of fairness. Maybe she was trying to let people know that she would not let our friendship interfere with her impartiality in choosing a team."

Reframing allows students to see situations without assigning negative motives or making destructive value judgments. It is a valuable tool for controlling feelings. Teachers can assist students with developing this skill by giving them "what if" scenarios to write about and/or discuss in small groups. Story starters can be offered that encourage students to look at an event from different perspectives. It takes practice, but it is a lifelong skill that will serve them well.

Motivating Oneself

> *We cannot always build the future for our youth,*
> *but we can build our youth for the future.*
> — Franklin D. Roosevelt (1940)

One of the most important characteristics to nurture in students is self-efficacy, the belief that they can influence their own thoughts and behavior. Earlier in this chapter I mentioned that we must help students understand that the only way they can change their feelings is to change their thought patterns. Discussion and practice are effective means for influencing their ability to take responsibility for their own feelings.

Building Resiliency

Another important component of intra-personal awareness is the concept of resiliency. Recent studies have examined why children of similar environments and experiences manifest such diverse abilities to thrive. This quality of personal resiliency has been attributed in large part to a person's ability to motivate herself or himself. While some are able to face great obstacles and failures and not lose their optimism, others are derailed by the slightest adversity. Teachers can be instrumental in reinforcing students' capable responses to difficulties.

Building Resilience (competency, belonging, usefulness, potency and optimism) requires these key experiences:

- provide students with authentic evidence of academic success
- show them that they are valued members of a community
- reinforce feeling that they have made a real contribution to their community
- make them feel empowered

— Sagor, 1996

Attribution Theory

Teachers have to take some of the responsibility for contributing to students' misconception that they are unable to control their futures. When teachers tell students how talented and gifted they are, they are actually undermining student success. What this inadvertently communicates to students is that their ultimate success is based on something beyond their control such as an innate talent. That is not the message educators need to be sending.

Major research on attribution theory was done by Wilson and Linville (1982). Attribution theory refers to those causal agents which people feel contribute to or interfere with their success on certain tasks. The researchers found that, in general, people attribute their accomplishment or lack of it to one of four things: the difficulty of the task, luck, innate ability/talent, or effort. The researchers point out that the first three factors are externally controlled. If students believe that their lack of success was based on the difficulty of the task, chance, or an inherited aptitude they are in essence denying any power over the situation. Similarly, if they attribute others' successes to these same factors they are likely to stop trying because they perceive that nothing they can do will influence the final results. Only one factor, effort, is internally controlled. Students who believe they can influence their achievements by their own efforts are far more likely to feel empowered and optimistic.

Teachers need to be cautious about their word choices. Let's say a teacher says to a student in class, "Jeremy, you are such a gifted artist. You have so much talent! Wow! I would never be able to draw like that. You are really lucky to have that ability."

What has just been communicated to Jeremy, and everyone else within hearing distance, is that the only way to be able to produce quality drawings is to be naturally gifted. If students feel that they are not blessed with such an ability, why should they try?

These words would be much better: "Jeremy, you must be so proud of your work. How long did it take you to do that? Wow! You really spent a lot of time and effort on that, didn't you? That just shows what can happen when you really put your heart and soul into something."

With the above statements the teacher has empowered everyone in the room by what was said and by what was implied—most things are possible with hard work. That is definitely a message educators want to send to students.

Something to Hope for

Schools that subtly (or sometimes not so subtly) tell children they will never amount to anything are robbing them of one of the most critical fundamentals all students need. They need hope; everyone does. It is incredibly paradoxical to see educators, who clearly communicate to their students that they are doomed to failure, become bewildered when their students won't try anymore. Would you?

When I was a child my mother gave me a small card that had the following saying:

Essentials For Happiness
Something to love
Something to do
Something to hope for

As long as I can remember, I have had those words posted somewhere close so that I can read them often. These three maxims have powerful implications for educators as they plan curriculums and environments designed to promote life values for students. In building classroom communities, educators must foster a loving environment, pay close attention to what students are asked to do, and be sure that students always have something to hope for.

Recognizing Emotions in Others

A teacher can help students learn to treat each other well. A good place to start is with building awareness. To learn empathy, a person must first be conscious of how the other person is feeling. In socially inept children, one of the basic characteristics they lack is the ability to use nonverbal language effectively. Some students (like Bryan in the earlier scenario) are unable to read and express emotion in facial expressions, gestures, personal space, postures, tone and loudness of voice, dress, and personal grooming. These inappropriate social behaviors are attributable to dyssemia, a difficulty in reading or expressing signs. Often underneath the out-of-sync exterior are intelligent, well-meaning children who are puzzled by their peers' rejection.

Students can learn to read emotions from another person's face, which is a lesson in empathy. Practice sessions whereby students are encouraged to both model emotions as well as interpret others' emotions are helpful in getting them to be more conscious of others' feelings. They can practice pantomiming as well as reading the seven universal facial expressions: anger, fear, sadness, disgust, surprise, happiness, and embarrassment. Teachers can ask students to watch videos with the sound turned off as they work in groups to infer what the characters are likely feeling. As students become more empathetic, they develop appropriate thinking patterns and hopefully learn to model care and concern for all living things.

Handling Relationships

Children Need:

- to Love
- to Be Loved
- to Feel Valued

When children feel secure, at ease, and happy they are less likely to act out, be destructive, or harm others. A caring classroom community can help them feel safer, calmer, and more joyful. Without question, teachers must model respectful behavior and a considerate attitude towards students. In order to feel secure, students must feel loved and valued. An interesting caveat to that maxim is that, in order to be emotionally healthy, children must also be able to give love. Building a caring classroom community requires that students are involved in the process of both giving and receiving caring and respect.

Teachers often worriedly comment on how quickly social skills seem to be deteriorating among today's school children. (For clarification on a part of the problem, I invite them to watch the behavior of their students' parents at ball games, assemblies, and the like). Students' cavalier treatment of one another appears to be escalating. Distrust, lack of respect, and even contempt are often exhibited in student interactions. Caring classrooms cannot exist where such antisocial behavior pervades.

Corporate America has sent a clear message to schools that they want students to be taught to think independently and also be able to work cooperatively on teams. Not only do teachers have to teach students how to think creatively, they have to teach children how to interact with one another. Students need to learn to be "people smart." They can learn the requisite skills, but it takes time and deliberate planning on the part of schools in general and teachers in particular.

Many teachers plan their classroom management programs around a focus on a more involved community of classmates. They use team-building activities (see *Fire Up! for Learning* by Thompson and VanderJagt) that build trust, interdependence, and involvement. One of the first things I do with new classes is insist that they learn each other's names and something about each other. In the Name Game on the following page, have each student complete a mini-autobiography card with questions such as these (or use your own).

Drumming to the Beat of a Different Marcher

Name Game

WHO IS THIS? _____

   a. What are your favorite things to do?

   _____

   _____

   b. What is something interesting about you that no one in this class knows about?

   _____

   _____

   c. Where have you lived besides here?

   _____

   _____

   d. What is the most unusual thing you have ever done or seen?

   _____

   _____

   e. What do people in this room need to know about you?

   _____

   _____

   f. What kind of music do you like?

   _____

   _____

   g. What's your favorite TV show? _____

Type up each set of information without putting the name with it. Hand out the sheets of collected data and tell students their first assignment is to match the names of their classmates to the information. I usually hand them a separate list of their classmates' names to help with correct spelling. This activity can also be handed out for homework so that students will talk to each other on the bus, in the hall, and outside of (as well as inside) the classroom.

BALL / BALLOON TOSS

Stand students in a circle. Have a person toss a whiffle ball across the circle. The receiver has to name the person who threw them the object. This game's more fun if you do it outside on a hot day with a water balloon!

TO TELL THE TRUTH

Have students introduce themselves by saying their names and three statements about themselves. Two of the statements must be true and one is a total lie. Other students must guess which statement is the lie. This is a great way to introduce a lesson on observations and inferences, facts and fiction, or other curriculum objectives.

Ways to Reinforce Name Use in the Classroom

- If you have the money to buy film, take a photograph of each class member. Make a poster with everyone's picture and name. Use the pictures for various activities and reviews.

- Require that students use each other's names when addressing one another. You do it, too. (e.g. I think that was a good point, Mark. What did Sheila say? May I do it after Shameka? Randy and Thomas have already had a turn, may I go next?)

- Give bonus points on tests, homework, etc. by pointing to a certain student and having the others write down his or her name.

- Let the students make a triangle card stand (a tri-folded piece of card stock) that have their names on them. Students may decorate them any way they like, but must display them during all discussions, activities, etc. Sometimes you may want to mix them up and get a volunteer to place them in their correct places (you can time it and make a contest of it if you like).

- Don't accept the pronouns "he" or "she" from anyone until they first correctly identify the person to whom they are referring.

Later, I teach students activities such as the "Car Wash." They are often the ones who come to me and whisper that a certain classmate is in need of a car wash. They sometimes initiate their own car washes when I am not even around.

The Car Wash

The Car Wash consists of simply lining up your class or group in two parallel lines quite close together. Then one student is sent through the wash (between the lines) and everyone touches her or him and says words of praise, affection, and encouragement. The pats on the back, hand-shaking, and verbal support produce a sparkling, shiny, happy "car" at the end of the wash!

We usually run one or two people through the car wash at a time rather than everybody in one big clean-up. That ensures that the responses of the washers are fresh, personal, and enthusiastic.

Adapted from *100 Ways to Enhance Self-Concepts in the Classroom.*
Canfield and Wells, 1976.

Drumming to the Beat of a Different Marcher

One day, I was having a really terrible, horrible, no good, very bad day at school. I was called to the office, and when I returned to my class my sixth graders had lined themselves up to give me a car wash. Needless to say my horrid day quickly became one of my greatest days as well as one of my fondest memories.

A common problem with low E.I. kids is that they refuse to acknowledge or sincerely apologize for their words and actions that hurt other people. Just as Bryan tried to dismiss his hurtful remark to Charlotte as, "I was just kidding with her," many students fail to understand the cost of their aggression. A really enlightening activity to use to help students address this issue is IALAC. This exercise has been around for years, but I first learned of it in Canfield and Wells' book, *100 Ways to Enhance Self-Concepts in the Classroom.*

IALAC

Each student is given a piece of paper on which are written in big letters, IALAC. They are told that the letters stand for this phrase, "I Am Lovable and Capable." Explain to students that everyone in class arrived that day with a certain amount of feelings regarding their lovableness and capableness. No one in the classroom has a right to do anything that diminishes another's capacity. Inform them that taking away someone's capacity for feeling lovable and capable can happen with words, a look, or a gesture. For the duration of the activity (usually a day) students are to carry around or wear their signs. Each time they feel that someone has done something diminishing, they are to tear off a piece of their sign (little chunks for small infractions and larger chunks for really hurtful things) and give it to the offender. The offender can do nothing but accept and keep the paper. At the end of the activity students discuss how it feels to be disrespected as well as how it feels to have to accept the pieces of signs from others.

Tips

- It is helpful to role-play the activity as a demonstration with the whole class before beginning the activity.

- Do not send students out of the class with their signs without consulting other adults in the school. (I once had a furious teacher walk in my room with a handful of pieces of paper demanding to know why my students were giving her parts of their signs. I tried not to giggle as I explained the activity. Boy, was she mad!)

- A great follow-up to this activity is teaching students how to make a sincere apology. It is empowering to students to learn to accept responsibility for their actions and know how to truly make amends for their misdeeds.

For great program models of social learning already in place look at the advisory programs promoted by the National Middle School Association, The Child Development Project (Lewis, Schaps, and Watson, 1996), or any number of the character education curricula being put in place for students K–12. Each of these programs uses prescribed activities and that foster positive interpersonal communication skills in students.

Curriculum Connections

> "... Deep down we all know that assemblies, classroom posters, and happy face stickers cannot change a student's attitude toward school or life outside of school. On the other hand, infusing the classroom and the curriculum with resiliency-building experiences can have a profound impact on students' self-images."
>
> – Richard Sagor (1996)

Finally, when building caring classrooms, social learning is ineffective when it is taught as a stand-alone, twice-a-week, or special exploratory unit. It has to be integrated across the curriculum and the school culture. It should be as valued as the cognitive standards and should be supported by the way classes are structured and the subject matter is taught.

Robert Sylwester (1995) suggests these ways to integrate social learning into the curriculum:

1. Using metacognitive activities

2. Using activities that promote social interaction

3. Using activities that provide emotional context

4. Avoiding emotional stress

5. Recognizing the relationship between emotions and health

> *A learning space needs to be hospitable not to make learning painless, but to make the painful things possible . . . things like exposing ignorance, testing tentative hypothesis, challenging false or partial information, and mutual criticism of thought. [None of these] can happen in an atmosphere where people feel threatened or judged.*
>
> *– Parker J. Palmer (1983)*

Coherent connections between social learning and subject matter learning can be made in natural, meaningful ways. Within their daily and unit lesson plans teachers of all disciplines can intentionally reinforce:

- Self-awareness
- Personal decision-making
- Managing feelings
- Handling stress
- Empathy
- Communications
- Self-disclosure
- Insight
- Self-acceptance
- Personal responsibility
- Assertiveness
- Group dynamics
- Conflict Resolution

Eric Jenson (1998) agrees that emotional literacy can be enhanced across the curriculum if all teachers would have students work together to make public group presentations, participate in local apprenticeships, and do community service-learning projects. He also supports having schools and classes do more celebrations, use more purposeful physical rituals, and concentrate on novel or controversial situations to engage student interest. He believes that social learning must be embedded in assignments, class structure, discipline choices, and purposeful outcomes.

Why Changing Thinking Patterns Is Important
- Thoughts Lead to Acts
- Acts Lead to Habits
- Habits Lead to Character
- Character Changes Destiny

Emotionally healthy classrooms go beyond establishing a safe and secure environment for all. They are places where there is a shared sense of wonder, joy, humor, and playfulness. Some fear that laughter signals a loss of control, an environment of chaos. Not so. Laughter is a softening influence that helps maintain attention levels, builds rapport, promotes creativity, increases motivation, and boosts retention. Compassionate humor can add to feelings of belonging as well as create a joy in learning. Students are in dire need of having the joy of learning returned to them.

> *With all our science can one tell how it is, or whence it is, that light comes into the soul?*
> – Henry David Thoreau

Emotional intelligence is also about more than the students. Teachers and staff members need to have time to purposefully build their own sense of community and their own sense of selves. Some say that the average child laughs hundreds of times a day, but the average adult laughs only a dozen times. That's a shame because research on laughter has proven that it relaxes your body, lowers your blood pressure, boosts your immune system, shuts off stress hormones, gives you perspective, and helps you take yourself less seriously. Everyone needs a good dose of humor and playfulness at least once a day. Educators should work on their own lightheartedness and help others find their own sense of inner joy.

After several of us were lamenting the dreaded bus duty (on the few weeks of absolutely miserable cold weather we have in the South), I wrote the following poem and sent it to my teacher buddies. We were still cold and aggravated that we had to do bus duty, but at least we could laugh about it.

Duty Calls

By Debbie Silver

You don your flannel underwear,
Roll on three pairs of socks.
You finally find your mukluks,
And take them from their box.

You wear two pairs of woolen slacks,
A sweater and a shirt.
You add a pair of knitted gloves,
And earmuffs wouldn't hurt!

You slip into your down-filled coat,
Pull on your fur-lined cap.
You pocket Liquid Sterno™ cans,
And last, your muffler wrap.

Now dressed, you join the family,
And meet their snickering stares.
They call you "Nanook of the North"
And fall out from their chairs.

You toss your nose into the air
And guess they'll never learn
What are the bare necessities . . .
When BUS DUTY'S your turn!

Recommended Reading List

Goleman, David. *Emotional Intelligence.* NY: Bantam Books, 1995.

Kessler, Rachael. *The Soul of Education: Helping Students Find Connection, Compassion, and Character at School.* Alexandria, VA: Association for Supervision and Curriculum Development (ASCD), 2000.

Loomans, Diana, et al. *The Laughing Classroom: Everyone's Guide to Teaching with Humor and Play.* Tiburon, CA: H.J. Kramer, Inc., 1993.

Sylwester, Robert. *A Celebration of Neurons: An Educator's Guide to the Human Brain.* Alexandria, VA: Association for Supervision and Curriculum Development (ASCD), 1995.

Thompson, Randy, and Dorothy VanderJagt. *Fire Up! For Learning: Active Learning Projects and Activities to Motivate and Challenge Students.* Nashville: Incentive Publications, 2002.

Thompson, Randy, and Dorothy VanderJagt. *Wow! What a Team.* Nashville: Incentive Publications, 2001.

Pay It Forward

But I'm Not Even Through Paying Back My Student Loans!

Teacher Surprise
by Debbie Silver

Monday morning lunch money
Is waiting for collection;
Christy's note from mommy says
To check for eye infection.

The office needs your tax form;
The pledge is yet unspoken.
Wendy's at your desk in tears,
Her new school bag is broken.

"You have a brand new student,"
The voice says from the speaker;
You're not done yet with grading sheets,
This deadline is a "squeaker."

School pictures are delivered,
They're needing to be sorted.
And textbook inventories;
RIGHT NOW must be reported!

Cheerleaders are selling tags,
But wait—the roll's not taken!
And the "sub" across the hall,
Yells, "Help, I feel forsaken!"

Larry needs his medicine,
And Craig must have a tissue.
Parents waiting in the hall
To see you on an issue.

The secretary calls you
For classroom count by races.
Kathy screams that Billy Roy
Tied knots in her shoelaces.

And as this nightmare worsens
Your heart now ceases beating
As someone with her clipboard
Walks in and asks for seating.

"I am your supervisor,"
  She says in salutation.
"Here today for annual
  Teacher Evaluation."

Drumming to the Beat of a Different Marcher

It's Not Just About the Test Scores

Teaching is an incredibly demanding profession. Teachers have to attend to a room full of different marchers while trying to dance to the beat of all kinds of drummers. Someone once likened teaching a roomful of students to "trying to change a flat tire on a moving vehicle." It can get a little harrowing at times. Added to this already overwhelming job is the burden of dealing with a national frenzy for the high-stakes-test-sweepstakes (Popham, 2001).

In June 2002, Secretary of Education Rod Paige issued a 66-page report blasting the teaching profession for being too concerned with how to teach and not concerned enough with what to teach. His implication is that schools can improve their test scores by hiring subject matter experts rather than graduates with education degrees. Raising test scores seems to be his main area of concern.

Somehow policymakers have finally convinced most of the public that children are better served by the administration of national achievement tests, the ranking of the results, and the comparison among schools for top scores. They have sold the idea that educators only need to assess what is easily measured (standardized objective tests covering isolated skills and facts) rather than examining more deeply what is actually going on with students.

High stakes tests results are being misused to perpetuate the myth that higher test scores are synonymous with better teaching. But what about the long-range character building and life skills teachers provide for students? Where does that get included? What about the student who takes an alternate route to success? When is that success balanced against his or her low scores on the 4th grade achievement test? What about the student who takes a little longer to "get ready" for the next level? Does his or her delay in achievement count against the 7th grade teacher or the 8th grade teacher? Who gets credit for his or her ultimate accomplishment? Determining what is effective teaching is just not as simple as the "quick fix" sages out there would have the public believe.

Furthermore, how does one address the dilemma of the teacher who shrewdly coaches the students on how to make better test scores but in the process destroys their love for that particular subject or their likelihood of being intellectually curious lifelong learners? For an in-depth assessment (pardon the pun) of what America's obsession with high stakes testing is doing to the educational system, I recommend that you read James Popham's book, *The Truth About Testing: An Educator's Call to Action*.

To improve schools, educators must address both the heart and the art of teaching. When I supervise teachers' classrooms I look at their students' test scores along with their students' products as a piece of the overall picture. I watch the teacher interact with the students, and I note how students interact with each other. I ask to look at written notes from the teacher to the students as well as the students' notes to their teacher (or Valentines, pictures, cards, etc.). I interview the students and ask them what it feels like to be in that class. Only by examining both quantitative data and qualitative information am I able to tell whether or not good teaching is happening. All classroom evaluators should follow the same procedure. It is not just about the scores.

Pay It Forward, the Movie

In the movie *Pay It Forward*, a middle school social studies teacher asks his students to come up with a plan for improving the world. Twelve-year-old Trevor McKinney takes the assignment to heart. He devises a scheme whereby he will do something totally selfless and helpful for three other people. Instead of expecting the recipients to pay him back, Trevor asks each one to "pay it forward" (i.e. do likewise for three other individuals). Mathematically the progression would be staggering, and very soon all would feel the world change.

The movie is extremely touching, and made me realize what it is that makes teachers so special. We pay it forward! Each and every day educators give away pieces of themselves to children. They invest their time, energy, and talent into these young individuals in the hope that someday they will "pay it forward" to the world. There is seldom any direct payback or even closure to the countless selfless acts educators make on behalf of children. Unlike standardized tests that give an instant (if highly unreliable) snapshot of a student's academic progress, there is no test to measure how successful educators have been in fulfilling their mission statements. It is an act of faith that educators continue to give and give with the expectation that they will somehow impact eternity. Educators do not talk about this aspect of the job enough. It is so much easier to get caught up in the mundane tasks of teaching than to look at the awesome responsibility and ultimate accountability teachers have to the future of the world. So, celebrate more! I would love to go into a teachers' lounge and hear someone say, "I think I touched a life today," or "I think I truly made a difference," or "You should have seen her face when her classmates gave her a standing ovation for her performance; I don't think she'll ever be the same again," or "Well, I think we can count those parents as our allies from now on."

I'm not quite sure why educators are so hesitant to acknowledge and celebrate their work. I once sold cosmetics door-to-door for a well-known company (mainly to finance my teaching habit), and when we had our sales meetings we cheered, we sang, we told success stories, and we generally bolstered each other in our attempts to make our sales quotas. They were wonderfully encouraging events. After my invigorating sales meeting on Monday nights I would go to school and have our Tuesday afternoon faculty meeting. What a contrast! All we did there was play the "Ain't it Awful?" and "You Think You've Got It Bad? Just Look at Me!" games. I simply couldn't get it out of my head that at the place where all the celebration was going on we were essentially talking about make-up, and at the place where we were virtually molding the future of our country, we did nothing but gripe and complain. That has got to change!

Faculty Meetings

Faculty meetings should be a place where teachers are encouraged to share their innovations, their triumphs, and their in-roads towards students' progress, their positive parent interactions, and the humorous things that occur in this intriguing field. If educators are to continue to pay it forward, they need to support one another, share their success stories, and to encourage one another in this most essential job. In her book, *If You Don't Feed the Teachers, They Will Eat the Students*, Dr. Neila Connors does an excellent job of outlining some very simple things administrators can do to foster such a climate.

Telling Our Stories

Educators who have taught for a while have stories about lives that have affected them and stories about lives that touched them as well. Those new to the profession will soon have their own narratives. In one of my presentations, *Be A Teacher—Be A Hero*, I give an account of David, a student I encountered during my first year of teaching. David was that child every teacher has experienced at least once. He was an "at risk" student before they had coined the term. His hostility and belligerence were exceeded only by his surly attitude and refusal to let me get near him.

I could have you weeping by telling you David's history, but I don't have to. You have seen or you will see children just like him. He did not have decent clothes, his teeth were not brushed, and usually he was not even clean. This child had witnessed more heartlessness in his seven years than most of us will see in a lifetime.

One of my colleagues told me not to get my feelings hurt by David's rejection of my attempts to get close to him. She told me that this child, like a lot of our students, was "emotionally bankrupt." She said that every adult he had ever loved or trusted had somehow hurt him or let him down. She told me that the only way he thought he could protect himself was to keep everyone at arm's length. I tried everything I knew to get close to David, but he was determined to antagonize me in every way he could manage. The beat he marched to was very, very far away. However, I was as stubborn as he was, so I kept on being his advocate and providing him with "tough love." It finally worked.

On my birthday after the other children went to lunch, David presented me with a very worn one-dollar bill. He said that his mother didn't own a car, so he had no way to get to a store. The dollar was his gift to me. Looking at his shabby clothes I almost gave the dollar back. But when I listened with more than my ears and saw the look of pride in his eyes, I took the bill and said, "David, thank you. This is exactly the right gift. I will treasure it always." He ran ahead of me to the lunchroom and proudly announced to my other students that they had all given me the wrong things—what I really liked was "cash money."

The two of us developed a relationship that lasted for years. As a teenager he was accused of committing a felony. When he was arrested he used his one phone call to contact me, his teacher, the person who had constantly said to him, "I'll always believe in you, and I'll always be here for you." Even though I couldn't prevent his being sentenced to hard labor at one of the toughest state penitentiaries in America, I was able to write to him throughout his incarceration, to voice my unconditional support for him, and to express my belief in his ultimate triumph.

When David earned his GED in prison, he mailed it to me with a note that said, "I did it all for you." Years later, he appeared in my driveway with his wife and two beautiful daughters. He told me he just wanted his family to meet me, the one person who believed in him—his teacher.

We all have such stories. It is usually the times we truly "drummed to the beat of our different marchers" that we most cherish because we realize that is when we were at our personal bests. In the movie *Pay It Forward* Trevor McKinney ponders why people hesitate to make the world a better place:

> *"I think some people are too scared or something to think things can be different . . . I guess it's hard for some people who are so used to things the way they are, even if they're bad, to change, because they kind of give up, and when they do, everybody loses."*

It's the same with teaching. Educators have to keep trying to do whatever works long-term. They have to be willing to change the things that do not work and keep searching to find the things that do. Do not give up. Continue to pay it forward. Educators have to drum to the beat of their different marchers because in the long run, that is what it is all about.

Recommended Reading List

Berg, Julie. *When a Classmate Dies.* Fargo, ND: Prairie House, Inc., 1991.

Connors, Neila A. *If You Don't Feed the Teachers, They Will Eat the Students! A Guide to Success for Administrators and Teachers.* Nashville: Incentive Publications, 2000.

Corrigan, Grace G. *A Journal for Christa: Christa McAuliffe, Teacher In Space.* Lincoln, NE: University of Nebraska Press, 1999.

Popham, W. James. *The Truth about Testing: An Educator's Call To Action.* Alexandria, VA: Association for Supervision and Curriculum Development (ASCD), 2001.

Johnson, Dale D., and Bonnie Johnson. *High Stakes: Children, Testing, and Failure in American Schools.* Lanham, MD: Rowman & Littlefield Publishers, Inc., 2002.

Glossary

Accommodation

Concept used by Piaget to describe the adjustment an individual makes when incorporating new information. Accommodation is the individual's response to the immediate and compelling informational input that has been and is being assimilated (see Assimilation).

Aggressive

Showing a readiness or having a tendency to attack or do harm to others.

Anchoring

Using a conditioned response to elicit a behavior (i.e. eating foods to feel comfort; thinking of a beautiful beach to bring on a sense of calm; listening to a song to feel energetic).

Assertive

Confident in stating your position or aim; forceful.

Assertive Discipline

An American theory based on a rigid set of rules, penalties and rewards. A simple set of rewards is displayed in every classroom, along with a list of rewards for keeping them and the consequences of breaking them.

Assimilation

Concept used by Piaget to describe the process of conceptualizing and internalizing one's new experience. Piaget believes that assimilation is a spontaneous process on the part of the child. (Used in conjunction with accommodation).

Attribution Theory

In the context of student motivation this theory suggests that students base their explanations of success on external causes (task difficulty, luck, innate ability) or internal causes (effort) or some combination of the four.

Automaticity

Learned behavior that has been so internalized that it can be done without thought or intention thus freeing the mind to do Higher-Order tasks.

Classical Conditioning

Term used to describe Pavlov's research on the pairing of a conditioned response with an unconditioned stimulus over time to see if the conditioned stimulus alone could trigger a response. In his classic experiment, he played a tone as he presented meat powder to a dog over and over. Eventually the tone alone (without the meat powder) resulted in the dog's beginning to salivate.

Constructivism

A perspective that holds that knowledge is constructed in the minds of learners based on their prior knowledge and previous experience.

Cooperative Learning

An instructional strategy that uses small groups of students working together and helping one another to complete a collaborative learning task.

Discrepant Event

A perplexing situation that causes cognitive dissonance (inability to understand). Like a magic trick that seems impossible.

Disequilibration

Term used by Piaget to describe the cognitive dissonance that occurs when what a child observes is inconsistent with his or her prior knowledge and/or beliefs.

Dyssemia

A difficulty in understanding nonverbal signs and signals.

Equilibration

Term used by Piaget to describe the motivational force for arriving at an adjustment between the twin concepts of assimilation and accommodation.

Drumming to the Beat of a Different Marcher

Extrinsic Rewards

Rewards that come from an outside source such as the teacher. Rewards include the obvious bonuses such as prizes, certificates, special privileges, gold stars, stickers, candy, gum, redeemable tokens, grades, or even money. Teacher praise is also considered to be an extrinsic reward as are more subtle signs of approval such as "thumbs up": signals, smiles, nods, hugs, and pats on the back.

Flow State

Term coined by Mihalyi Csikszentmihalyi to describe a state of concentrated action and awareness.

Intrinsic Rewards

Rewards as the inherent or natural consequences of the behavior. Some researchers prefer the term reinforcers to rewards because teacher use them to strengthen behavior (make it more likely to be repeated).

Learning Cycle

A teaching strategy that enables students to construct learning for themselves through the exploration phase, the concept development phase, and the concept application phase. All phases are contingent on effective teacher questioning.

Lounge Lizards

Negative school personnel who sometimes take over the teacher's lounge. They are known by their disgruntled attitudes, their incessant gossip, their snipes at others, and their lack of tolerance for anything new or different.

Misconceptions

Faulty understanding of a concept. Naive ideas.

No-tolerance Policy (Zero-tolerance Policy)

Zero tolerance—the phrase says exactly what it means: no second chances, no mistakes, no questions, no ifs, ands, or buts. Under many zero-tolerance policies, bringing a plastic knife to school for a lunch is equivalent to bringing a switchblade, and giving a friend aspirin is the same as selling narcotics. Since they are considered equal, so is the punishment—no questions asked.

Performance-contingent Rewards

Rewards that are available only when the student achieves a certain standard (i.e. anyone who makes at least 95% on a homework assignment gets a sticker.)

PETA

People for the Ethical Treatment of Animals. www.peta-online.org/

Public Law 94.142

The Education for All Handicapped Children Act. Passed in 1975, it calls for an Individualized Education Program (IEP) for each child with disabilities. It is a Federal law which requires all learners with disabilities are educated in the "least restrictive environment."

Reframing

The ability to see events from another perspective.

Resiliency

Ability to recover quickly from setbacks.

Request for Proposals (RFP)

Documents from grant awarding institutions defining their purpose along with the rules and the process needed in order to obtain their funds. Typically, the institution's evaluators identify those proposals capable of delivering the required results.

Self-efficacy

The belief that one can influence his or her own thoughts and behavior.

Sponge Activity

A short activity designed to "soak up" time that would otherwise be wasted in the classroom. It can be used as "bell ringer" work given at the beginning of a period to engage students when they enter the classroom. Other uses are for the end of class, for unexpected interruptions, or for transitional time during class.

Success-contingent Rewards

Rewards that are given for good performance and might reflect either success or progress towards a goal (i.e. either you make 100% on this test or you improve your last score by 5%).

Task-contingent Rewards

Rewards that are available to students for merely participating in an activity without regard to any standard of performance (i.e. anyone who turns in a homework paper gets an "A").

Tourette's Syndrome

A chronic, physical disorder of the brain which causes both motor tics and vocal tics, and begins before the age of eighteen.

Type A Personality

Manifested behavior characterized by an intense sustained drive to achieve goals and an eagerness to compete. Persons categorized as Type A tend to have a persistent desire for external recognition and advancement.

Type B Personality

Manifested behavior is usually defined as the absence of Type A behavior. Persons categorized as Type B tend to be relaxed, accepting, at ease, patient, and generally content. They are at peace with themselves and others.

Wait Time

Term applied to describe the interval between the time a teacher asks a question and a learner responds.

"With-it-ness"

A teacher's ability to monitor what is going on in a classroom and be able to act on inappropriate behavior by redirecting it before it is further disruptive.

Zone of Proximal Development

The distance between one's present developmental level and the level of potential future development (e.g. one that is reasonably attainable and yet just far enough beyond easy reach to sustain interest—somewhere between anxiety and boredom).

Bibliography

Armstrong, Thomas. *Awakening Genius in the Classroom.* Alexandria, VA: Association for Supervision and Curriculum Development (ASCD), 1998.

Armstrong, Thomas. *MIs in the Classroom.* Alexandria, VA: Association for Supervision and Curriculum Development (ASCD), 1994.

Bandura, Albert. Human Agency in Social Cognitive Theory. *American Psychologist* 44 (1175–1184), 1989.

Breeden, Terri, and Emalie Egan. *Positive Classroom Management.* Nashville: Incentive Publications, 1997.

Brogan, P. A Parent's Perspective: Educating the Digital Generation. *Educational Leadership* 58 (2), 57–59, 2000.

Brophy, Jere E., Ed. *Advances in Research on Teaching.* Greenwich, CT: JAI Press, 1989.

Canter, Lee, and Marlene Canter. *Lee Canter's Assertive Discipline: Positive Behavior Management for Today's Classroom.* Santa Monica: Lee Canter & Associates, 1992.

Canfield, J., and H. C. Wells. *100 Ways to Enhance Self-Concepts in the Classroom.* Englewood Cliffs, NJ: Prentice-Hall, 1976.

Carnegie, Dale. *How to Stop Worrying and Start Living.* NY: Simon & Schuster, 1948.

Chance, P. The Rewards of Learning. *Phi Delta Kappan* 74 (3), 200–207, 1992.

Checkley, K. The First Seven . . . and the Eighth. *Educational Leadership* 55 (1), 8–13, 1997.

Connors, Neila A. *If You Don't Feed the Teachers, They Eat the Students!* Nashville, Incentive Publications, Inc., 2000.

Covey, Stephen R. *The Seven Habits of Highly Effective People.* NY: Simon & Schuster, 1989.

Csikszentmihalyi, Mihalyi. *Flow: The Psychology of Optimal Experience.* NY: Harper & Row, 1990.

Curwin, Richard L., and Allen Mendler. *Discipline with Dignity.* Alexandria, VA: Association for Supervision and Curriculum Development (ASCD), 1988.

DeJong, C., & J. Hawley. Making Cooperative Learning Groups Work. *Middle School Journal* 26 (4), 45–48, 1995.

Forte, Imogene, and Sandra Schurr. *The Cooperative Learning Guide & Planning Pak for Middle Grades.* Nashville, Incentive Publications, Inc., 1992.

Forte, Imogene, and Sandra Schurr. *Standards-Based Math Graphic Organizers.* Nashville: Incentive Publications, Inc., 2001.

Forte, Imogene, and Sandra Schurr. *Standards-Based Science Graphic Organizers.* Nashville: Incentive Publications, Inc., 2001.

Forte, Imogene, and Sandra Schurr. *Standards-Based Social Studies Graphic Organizers.* Nashville: Incentive Publications, Inc., 2001.

Middleton, J.A., et al. Shopping for Technology. *Educational Leadership* 55 (3). 20–23, 1997.

Gardner, Howard. *Frames Of Mind: The Theory Of MIs.* NY: Basic Books, 1983.

Gardner, Howard. Reflections on MIs: Myths and Messages. *Phi Delta Kappan* 77 (3), 200–203. 206–209, 1995.

Gregorc, Anthony G. *An Adult's Guide to Style.* Columbia, CT: Gregorc Associates, Inc., 1982.

Hatch, T. (1997). Getting Specific about MIs. *Educational Leadership* 54 (6), 26–29, 1997.

Healy, Jean M. *Failure to Connect: How Computers Affect Our Children's Minds—For Better and Worse.* NY: Simon & Schuster, 1998.

Jensen, Eric. *Teaching with the Brain in Mind.* Alexandria, VA: Association for Supervision and Curriculum Development (ASCD), 1998.

Jung, Carl (H.G. Baynes, Trans). *Psychological Types.* NY: Harcourt, Brace & Co, 1923.

Kagan, Jerome M., et al. *Galen's Prophecy: Temperament in Human Nature.* NY: Basic Books, 1994.

Kellough, R.D., and N. G. Kellough. *Middle School Teaching: A Guide to Methods and Resources.* Columbus, OH: Merrill, 1999.

Kohn, Alfie. *Beyond Discipline: From Compliance to Community.* Alexandria, VA: Association for Supervision and Curriculum Development (ASCD), 1996.

Kohn, Alfie. *Punished by Rewards: The Trouble with Gold Stars, Incentive Plans, A's, Praise, and Other Bribes.* Boston: Houghton Mifflin, 1993.

Kounin, Jacob S. *Discipline and Group Management in Classrooms.* Melbourne, FL: Krieger Publishing, 1977.

Lewis, C.C., Schaps, E., and M.S. Watson. The Caring Classroom's Academic Edge. *Educational Leadership* 54 (2). 16–21, 1996.

Littauer, Florence. *Your Personality Tree.* Dallas: Word Publishing, 1986.

Lytle, J. H. The Inquiring Manager—Developing New Leadership Structures to Support Reform. *Phi Delta Kappan* 77, 664–670, 1996.

Maslow, Abraham H. *Motivation and Personality.* NY: Addison-Wesley, 1954.

Nagy, Allen, and Geraldine Nagy. *How to Raise Your Child's Emotional Intelligence: 101 Ways to Bring Out the Best in Your Children and Yourself.* Bastrop, TX: Heartfelt Publications, 1999.

Newmann, F. M., H. Marks, and A. Gamoran. Authentic Pedagogy: Standards that Boost Student Performance. *Issues in Restructuring Schools* 8, 1–11, 1995.

O'Neil, J. On Emotional Intelligence: A Conversation with Daniel Goleman. *Educational Leadership* 54, (01). 6–11, 1996.

Palmer, Parker J. *To Know As We Are Known: A Spirituality of Education.* San Francisco: HarperCollins, 1983.

Piaget, Jean. *To Understand Is to Invent.* NY: Viking Press, 1974.

Purkey, William W. *Self-Concept And School Achievement.* Englewood Cliffs, NJ: Prentice-Hall, 1970.

Randolph, C. H., and C.M. Everston. Images of Management for Learner-Centered Classrooms. *Action in Teacher Education* 16(1) 55–63, 1994.

Sagor, R. Building Resiliency in Students. *Educational Leadership* 54 (2). 38–43, 1996.

Silver, Debbie. Engaging Students in the Learning Cycle. *Principal,* 77 (4), 62–64,1998.

Silver, Harvey F.,and M.J. Perini. *So Each May Learn: Integrating Learning Styles And MIs.* Alexandria, VA: Association for Supervision and Curriculum Development (ASCD), 2000.

Sylwester, Robert. *A Celebration of Neurons: An Educator's Guide to the Human Brain.* Alexandria, VA: Association for Supervision and Curriculum Development (ASCD), 1995.

Thompson, Randy, and Dorothy VanderJagt. *Fire UP! for Learning.* Nashville: Incentive Publications, Inc., 2002.

Tomlinson, Carol A. *The Differentiated Classroom: Responding To The Needs Of All Learners.* Alexandria, VA: Association for Supervision and Curriculum Development (ASCD), 1999.

Vatterrot, C. Student-Focused Instruction: Balancing Limits with Freedom in the Middle Grades. *Middle School Journal* 28 (2), 28–38, 1995.

Vygotsky, L. *Mind In Society: The Development of Higher Psychological Process.* Cambridge: Harvard University Press, 1978.

Wittrock, Merlin C., Ed. *Handbook of Research on Teaching.* Englewood Cliffs, NJ: Merrill/Prentice Hall, 1986.

Wilson, T.D., and P.W. Linville. Improving Academic Performance of College Freshmen: Attribution Theory Revisited. *Journal of Personality of Social Psychology* 42, 367–376, 1982.